SOMEHOW IT WORKS

A Candid Portrait of the 1964 Presidential Election by

NBC NEWS

edited by

Gene Shalit and **Lawrence K. Grossman**

photographs by

David Hollander and **Paul Seligman**

Designed by John Graham

Doubleday & Company, Inc., Garden City, New York

I have just been informed that this portion of the Convention proceedings is being fed to Europe by satellite, and I have been asked to explain what is going on. I am afraid that is beyond my powers. It would be hard to explain it even to an American. As best as I can put it for Europeans, the Goldwater people, like those who will demonstrate later for other candidates, have been waiting for weeks and months and years to display in some outward, tangible way, how they feel about their candidate. When, finally, he was formally put in nomination, all of the pent-up energy, exuberance, noise, signs, slogans, bands and balloons suddenly were released. It is partly political, partly emotional, partly propaganda, partly a social mechanism, partly a carnival, and partly mass hysteria. It can be described as nonsense, and often is—but somehow it works.

DAVID BRINKLEY, AT THE REPUBLICAN CONVENTION, JULY 15, 1964

24997

This book has a two-fold aim. The photographs are a visual attempt to capture the flavor of an American Presidential election year — from the pre-primary period right through the final balloting. The text is a narrative of the events themselves — told largely in the at-the-scenes words of the political figures and NBC newsmen. The word-by-word narrative, of course, has been abridged, but every effort has been made to retain the flavor of the dialogue as it was spoken. □ The 1964 Presidential election story called for untold hours of television and radio time and the efforts of many hundreds of people working for NBC News. In addition to the reporters themselves, credit for the NBC News coverage of this election year must be given to a number of behind-the-scenes figures: Julian Goodman, Vice President of NBC News; Robert Northshield, General Manager; Reuven Frank, Executive Producer; Frank Jordan, Manager of NBC News' election planning; Chet Hagen, producer of the special campaign programs; George Murray, administrator of NBC News' Convention and election coverage; William Trevarthen and Charles Corcoran, who supervised the massive technical requirements for NBC's election year coverage; and Russell Tournabene and James Holton, in charge of NBC Radio coverage. □ For each of these men, there were scores of reporters, writers, researchers, political specialists, stringers, engineers, cameramen, secretaries and copy boys. It is only fitting to acknowledge the superb contribution of all these dedicated people in bringing broadcasting's most comprehensive coverage of the 1964 Presidential election year to the nation.

WILLIAM R. McANDREW

Executive Vice President in charge of NBC News

Contents

PHOTOGRAPHIC CREDITS: PAGE 224

PROLOGUE

Some of the peculiar flavor of American politics can be seen in a scrutiny of this one photograph, one of the millions of frozen images left to us from an election year. It describes an encounter on a snowy residential street in New Hampshire in February—the ground, the neat clapboard houses, the leafless white birch and the sky behind it all about the same color as the snow. In the whiteness of this cold and quiet small town a little color is welcome; and equally welcome in the quiet cold is the noisy warmth the visiting politician always brings with him. He brings it with him because he must, because the temper of our country demands it. This visitor, the hulking blackness on the right, is Governor Rockefeller, a multi-millionaire trying not to look like one. His overcoat is an old, belted-back model out of style for years. The others at the scene

wear gloves, but not the Governor. He is there to shake hands, and whatever it is that passes between two people in a handshake surely is diminished by two thicknesses of leather and wool. To the plump and well-fed little girl in the flowered parka, he offers: (1) A smile (His face is out of range, but how else could an American politician greet a child when her parents are there and the photographers around?); (2) His ungloved hand for shaking; (3) A box of animal crackers; and (4) In his coat pocket for cases of special need, a hand of bananas. Baby kissing is laughably old fashioned and unsanitary. (It also means they have to be lifted up off the ground, which is hard on a man's back in a long day of campaigning.) But animal crackers are boxed and cleanly wrapped, and bananas are immaculate and germ-free in their own skins—a requisite quality in a country that won't buy a detergent until it is warranted to clean whiter than white. Leftward, an older girl holding the poster is laughing gaily (she is out of school, and there is a little excitement in town), at the Governor's witticism. A small packet of such witticisms is essential, and can be used over and over. But the little girl in the parka is not quite old enough to get the joke, and the lady in the center didn't hear it because she is looking away and her ears are covered. The poster is the standard political graphic art—red, white and blue, the photograph showing the candidate smiling but not overdoing it (remember what happened to Adlai Stevenson's too many jokes and too many laughs). How many photographs of this Governor did they pick through before they chose this one? In the poster's lower right corner can be seen the printer's union label. Just try to run for President without that. Fully visible here are only two people old enough to vote, and so if Rockefeller's handshakes, jokes, animal crackers and bananas won him the hearts of everybody in sight, he would have moved just two 70-millionths of the way to the White House. As things turned out, he lost the New Hampshire primary to Lodge. Lodge lost the Republican nomination to Goldwater. And Goldwater lost New Hampshire to Johnson just nine months after this picture of a greeting by warm people in a cold town.

DAVID BRINKLEY

THE PRIMARIES

NEW HAMPSHIRE

December 22, 1963. The thirty days of official mourning for John Fitzgerald Kennedy have drawn to a close. The moratorium on politics is over. Ten days later, a Presidential election year begins.

In January, 1964, President Lyndon B. Johnson is at the height of his popularity. Public opinion polls show him with overwhelming leads over every possible Republican opponent. But, so far, only one Republican—Gov. Nelson A. Rockefeller of New York—has announced his candidacy for President. The Governor entered the race on November 7, 1963, two weeks before the assassination of President Kennedy. Speaking from Albany at 8:30 am—and seen nationally on the TODAY television program — Gov. Rockefeller made his formal announcement and revealed his first target would be the New Hampshire primary on March 10. Immediately after reading this statement, he flew to Nashua, N. H., where he said the same thing all over again. "I wanted to make this announcement myself, personally, here in New Hampshire," he said, promising to campaign "very actively" in that State.

The Governor's campaign has lacked the support of many influential Republicans, who doubt his ability to win in November because of his divorce and remarriage. So, moderate Republicans look beyond him to William Scranton, the popular Governor of Pennsylvania; to Henry Cabot Lodge, the Ambassador to Vietnam; to George Romney, the eloquent Governor of Michigan; and to former Vice President Richard Nixon, who came close to winning the Presidency in 1960. The one prominent Republican not on the moderates' list is the man who has already assembled more delegates than all the others combined—Sen. Barry M. Goldwater of Arizona, leader of the Republican Party's conservative forces.

For two years, Sen. Goldwater's supporters have waged a campaign in his behalf, hoping to persuade him to enter the race or—failing that—to draft him for the nomination. Now, three days into the new year, the Senator makes his move. On a bright, sunny Friday morning—January 3, 1964 —Sen. Goldwater faces reporters and television cameras on the patio of his home in Paradise City, on the edge of the desert near Phoenix, Arizona. "I will seek the Republican Presidential nomination," he declares, and he states a theme that will be heard again and again during the campaign: "I will not change my beliefs to win votes. I will offer a choice, not an echo. This will not be an engagement of personalities. It will be an engagement of principles... I am convinced that we must face up to our conscience... Let there be a choice right now, and in clear, understandable terms. And I ask all those who feel and believe as I

do to join with me in assuring both the choice and the victory." In a reference to Gov. Rockefeller, the Senator says he has "not heard from any announced Republican candidate a declaration of political principle that could possibly offer the voters a clear choice in the election." And he discloses that he, too, will enter the New Hampshire primary.

Gov. Rockefeller, in Portsmouth, N. H., says he is "genuinely pleased" that Sen. Goldwater has entered the race. But the Governor fires off a telegram to the Senator, challenging him to a face-to-face debate "on the issues" in New Hampshire. The Senator turns it aside, commenting, "I see no sense in Republicans berating other Republicans." The January New England air is filled with charges and counter-charges as the candidates trudge through the snow and sleet of New Hampshire's cities and hamlets.

ROCKEFELLER: Americans will not respond to a political creed that cherishes the past solely because it offers an excuse for shutting out the hard facts and difficult tasks of the present.

GOLDWATER: A choice between Johnson and Rockefeller would be a choice between Tweedle-Dum and Tweedle-Dee.

ROCKEFELLER: How can there be solvency when Goldwater is against the graduated income tax? How can there be security when he wants to take the United States out of the United Nations? How can there be sanity when he wants to give area commanders the authority to make decisions on the use of nuclear weapons?

GOLDWATER: Rockefeller believes in compulsory unions. I don't agree. The Governor believes in the Social Security approach to medical care for the aged. I don't. He believes in Federal aid to education below the college level. I disagree. He favors the limited test ban treaty. I oppose it.

After his first swing through the State, Sen. Goldwater is buoyed by the enthusiasm he sees for his candidacy. "If we can just keep this up, we'll have it made," he says. Meanwhile, other moderate Republicans are busy. A write-in campaign is launched by backers of Ambassador Lodge. A similar campaign gets under way for Mr. Nixon. Even Harold Stassen jumps in. Former President Dwight D. Eisenhower urges Gov. Scranton to make himself available for the Republican Presidential nomination, but the Governor holds out for "an honest draft."

Reminded that his boosters are working for him, the Governor says, "I've been doing a great deal to discourage them." And on January 27 there is another candidate: Sen. Margaret Chase Smith of Maine throws her chapeau into the ring. Appearing at the Women's National Press Club in Washington, Mrs. Smith cites many reasons for not entering the race. When the list is completed she says, "So, because of these very impelling reasons against my running, I have decided that [dramatic pause] I shall enter the New Hampshire and the Illinois primaries."

While the candidates campaign feverishly in New Hampshire, they are ever mindful of California, whose 86 delegates are at stake in the June 2 primary. So, from time to time, Sen. Goldwater and Gov. Rockefeller interrupt their New Hampshire schedules to jet to the West Coast for brief but intensive campaigning.

GOLDWATER [San Francisco]: The John Birch Society is far less a menace to the United States than the Americans for Democratic Action or the United Automobile Workers.

ROCKEFELLER [Los Angeles]: All signs point to a real successful campaign here.

Back in New Hampshire, Sen. Goldwater's campaign appears to fade as the winter deepens. Starting with an apparent four-to-one edge over Gov. Rockefeller, he now concedes he will be satisfied with 35 per cent of the vote. Mrs. Smith opens her quest for votes in the village of Pittsburg, N. H., in weather 29 degrees below zero. Gov. Rockefeller goes relentlessly on, apparently determined to shake every hand in the State. The Lodge write-in campaign begins to catch on. Gov. Rockefeller telephones him in Saigon, urging him to withdraw from the race. Sen. Goldwater attacks the Ambassador, charging that he has "balled things up" in Vietnam. Mindful of the trend, the Senator minimizes New Hampshire's importance. "The person who wins in California will be the Party's nominee," he predicts. New Hampshire primary day is Tuesday, March 10. On Saturday, March 7, Sen. Goldwater departs. "We've got it made," he says as he takes off for Washington. In the days before the State votes, NBC News reports from New Hampshire.

FRANK McGEE: There will be 1,308 delegates at the Republican Convention in July. Exactly 14 of these will come from New Hampshire. That is about one out of every 100. And even these 14, once they get to San Francisco, will not be bound to vote for the

winner of this primary. Figured that way, the amount of time, energy and money being spent here by a pack of Presidential candidates makes no sense at all, but candidates do not and cannot figure it that way. They have a far larger objective in mind. Because it holds the first primary in the nation, New Hampshire offers the candidates their first chance to prove that they can get votes. Consequently, no voters in the nation will be politicked more, or polled as much, as those who live in this small corner of New England. And no voters will enjoy the fuss being made over them more. Once every four years they have the satisfying feeling that they are shaping momentous events. They are, for although they have only a small voice in deciding the ultimate winner, they have a decisive voice in sorting out the losers.

Since it must begin somewhere, let it begin in New Hampshire. Small matter that the State is not a good laboratory to test their solutions for the nation's problems. A State with only three Negroes for every thousand population may not share the candidates' feeling of urgency about civil rights. So other issues must be found and stressed.

CHET HUNTLEY: New Hampshire's primary election lends continuity to an honorable process that began 60 years ago in Wisconsin during the Progressive administration of Gov. Robert M. LaFollette. He sought to take the nomination of Presidential candidates away from the machinations of professional politicians who dominated the national Conventions. LaFollette's primary election has worked: the smoke-filled room is an anachronism, and the candidates of the past 40 years, at least, have been popular choices. There will be 16 State primaries this year, and that is just about the right number—reflecting the good sense of the American voter. Fifty primaries would be impossible. No primaries would be worse.

MERRILL MUELLER: Politics comes naturally to many people, but few master the art of shaking hands with strangers in an attempt to turn them into voters. This gregarious blessing is one of Nel-

son Rockefeller's strongest assets. Whether it's in a bustling metropolis, or in a frozen village, the Governor campaigns as "Rocky, the regular guy." His blitz campaigning relies on the direct approach to men, women and children.

ROCKEFELLER: Hi, nice to have seen you.

BOY: Where are you going?

ROCKEFELLER: I'm going to a super market. Do you go shopping with your mommy? That's where I'm going.

BOY: Why?

ROCKEFELLER: Well, because I'm trying to get support to run for President of the United States.

BOY: Why?

ROCKEFELLER: Well, it's a good question. Because I'm worried about what's going on in the world and I want to do my part to help. That's why I'm doing it, so that nice boys like you will have a real chance to grow up in a country where there's freedom and where there's opportunity. And you are a wonderful boy.

ROBERT MacNEIL: Sen. Goldwater's campaign has been restrained. He seemingly prefers small, indoor groups to the more aggressive style of his rivals. He is not an easy man to advise. About the only concession he made was to eliminate the 'damns' and 'hells' which used to season his talks.

GOLDWATER: I'm not one of these hand-shaking candidates. And I don't kiss babies, because I lose track of their age too soon. And I don't like to insult the American intelligence by thinking that a loud whack on the back will get your vote.

MacNEIL: On two themes, Goldwater seems to touch a vibrant chord in many voters: opposition to big government and a call for a firm foreign policy. He feels that his basic proposition—a choice, not an echo—remains untested. Voters may put the proposition another way: Is Goldwater a desirable conservative or an undesirable extremist?

GOLDWATER: A conservative in America believes in building progress upon the proven values of the past. The conservatives are great students of history. They recognize that human nature has never changed; that man will react today precisely as

he reacted to problems two hundred or two thousand years ago.

McGEE: For the first time in the nation's political history, a woman is actively seeking the Presidential nomination of a major party. She is Margaret Chase Smith, a soft spoken Senator with a proven vote-getting ability. Mrs. Smith admits that she has an uphill battle, but does not consider that being a woman is one of her drawbacks. She is testing whether a candidate can make headway with little money, no organization, but lots of contact with people. She is best at meeting people on the streets. She is warm and friendly, as she chats with those she meets. In campaigning, she is an effective speaker, but everywhere the key question is about a woman running for President.

SEN. SMITH: I consider women people. And I think we should not choose our candidates because they are women or men. I think we should choose them because of their qualifications or lack of qualifications. I have had 23 years in the House and Senate. From the beginning, I took my place not as a woman Congressman, not as a woman Senator, but as a Congressman and as a Senator. I have never asked for any special privileges and I certainly never have gotten any. I think that if you talked with some of the members of the committees that I served on, you would find that the reputation I have is that Margaret Smith does her homework. She accepts and carries the responsibility that is hers and she acts for her State as a person, and not as a man or a woman.

McGEE: Another candidate is Harold E. Stassen. Stassen has held many important posts, both elective and appointive, but always the big goal has eluded him. In New Hampshire, he is in the race again. Since Stassen's campaign is not as big or colorful as some of the others, emphasis is placed on full-page newspaper advertisements that stress Stassen's rather complete political career. He was Governor of Minnesota at the age of thirty-one. He tried for the Presidential nomination in 1948 and 1952. In 1964, he is trying again.

20

In New Hampshire, the consent of a Presidential candidate is not required to put his name on the ballot, but he may request that his name be withdrawn. No such restrictions apply to a candidate's supporters if they decide to conduct a write-in campaign for him. That's the case of Henry Cabot Lodge, the 1960 Republican Vice Presidential nominee. He is now the Ambassador to Vietnam. New Hampshire borders on Massachusetts, Ambassador Lodge's home State. So, he is well known here. From his headquarters in Concord, there have been two mailings to 96,000 Republicans in the State. The first enclosed pledge cards, to be sent to Ambassador Lodge in Vietnam to indicate public support. The second included specimen ballots, marked to indicate how a voter could write in his name.

DAVID BRINKLEY: Ambassador Lodge has not tried very hard to discourage his candidacy. And that creates an awkward situation for the White House: the delicate and difficult Vietnamese policy being carried out by an ambassador who is running (or being run) for President in a campaign where Vietnam certainly will be an issue. President Johnson has said nothing in public, but some of his advisers think Lodge should either get out of the race decisively, or give up his job in Vietnam. So far he has done neither.

McGEE: The second write-in campaign here is for Richard Nixon. Nixon supporters in New Hampshire conduct rallies to gather write-ins for him. Heading the campaign is former Gov. Wesley Powell, a Republican maverick. Initially, Powell thought he would run himself, but he changed his mind and went for Nixon.

POWELL: Now let me tell you something. Richard Nixon has the only name known in every home, in every hamlet, in every city of our wonderful country. He is the best qualified, the most experienced, and he has the name which is known throughout the world.

McGEE: Four candidates—Sen. Goldwater, Gov. Rockefeller, Sen. Smith and Harold Stassen. Two non-candidates—Ambassador Lodge and Richard Nixon. And so, the stage is set for Tuesday.

*P*rimary day arrives with freezing temperatures, snow and sleet. Taking the storm in stride, New Hampshire's voters drive, walk, slip and slide to the polls. On March 10, primary election night, NBC-TV reports.

HUNTLEY: Stored in our computer are the past voting records and habits of every precinct, town and village of New Hampshire. In seven-millionths of a second, the machine can compare a fragment of today's voting with past voting returns and render a projection of the total outcome.

McGEE: By 7:25, this evening, it became clear that Ambassador Henry Cabot Lodge would win the New Hampshire primary. The RCA 301 Computer projected that the Ambassador would take as much as 35 per cent of the vote. As recently as last night, some of his campaign chieftains were saying privately that they'd be delighted with 15 per cent. It has been agreed by most candidates that any write-in for Lodge would eat into Rockefeller's vote, and that seems to be the case.

RAY SCHERER [In Washington, D.C.]: Here with me is Cliff White, director of field operations for Sen. Goldwater. The Senator said he hoped to get 40 per cent of the votes in New Hampshire. He is not getting it. What happened?

WHITE: Ambassador Lodge is, in effect, a regional individual. I don't think he can get the nomination, and I suspect that the people in New England are merely paying tribute to a native son.

McGEE: Campaign managers for Sen. Goldwater and Gov. Rockefeller are being left in the position of saying that the New Hampshire primary, where they had courted the vote so heavily, will actually prove nothing. Former New Hampshire Gov. Hugh Craig, a leader of the Rockefeller forces, is with NBC's Sander Vanocur in Concord.

SANDER VANOCUR: What do you think this election proves, so far as Gov. Rockefeller is concerned? Is he out of the Presidential race?

CRAIG: Gee, I don't see that at all. Gov. Rockefeller seems to be holding his own with Sen. Goldwater. He is our opposition, as far as I'm concerned. If

we can do well against him, we've got a victory.

VANOCUR: Did his divorce hurt Gov. Rockefeller?

CRAIG: I can't understand what you mean by being hurt. We're holding our own here, except against Lodge, and we haven't been running against Lodge. He hasn't been a candidate. He's not an opponent. He hasn't campaigned.

VANOCUR: Do you think that Gov. Rockefeller will now go on into all the rest of the primaries?

CRAIG: I'm certain he will. He is leaving tomorrow for California to start his campaign there.

McGEE: Our lady candidate, Sen. Margaret Chase Smith, has not done well in the returns so far. She is with NBC's Nancy Dickerson in Washington.

NANCY DICKERSON: How do you feel, Senator?

SEN. SMITH: Well, I'm very happy, but I'd be happier if I were getting more votes.

NANCY DICKERSON: Are you disappointed with the outcome so far?

SEN. SMITH: I wouldn't be human if I wasn't.

McGEE: The write-in campaign for Ambassador Lodge appears to have been sharply stimulated in the past three weeks by statements from his son, George Lodge, suggesting rather firmly that his father was a candidate even though he remained in Vietnam. The younger Lodge has now arrived from Boston and is now in Concord.

GEORGE LODGE: I think it is a wonderful vote of confidence in my father. I know he will be surprised and gratified when he hears about it. He regards his responsibility in Saigon right now as extremely serious. He was Ambassador during the crucial days of transition in Vietnam and he sees it as his duty to see it through. He is not one to pull out of a fight. However, if his Party calls on him in Convention, there is no doubt in my mind but that he will answer that call and do it gratefully, humbly, enthusiastically.

HERB KAPLOW: Nixon hopes the other men will cancel each other out, and that he will make respectable showings in the primaries he will not be able to duck. He seems to be holding his own tonight as a less aggressive write-in candidate than Lodge. Nixon is presenting himself as the best team player. He will do everything he can for the Party. Finally, Nixon presents himself as the middle-of-the-roader, the man whose political philosophy comes closest to a Republican consensus.

McGEE: Another campaign adding interest to the New Hampshire primary has been the late blooming write-in campaign for Robert Kennedy for the Democratic Vice Presidential slot. Gov. John W. King, who headed that campaign, talks to NBC.

VANOCUR: Governor, would you have been embarrassed if President Johnson received fewer votes tonight than Attorney General Robert Kennedy in the write-in ballot?

KING: I don't get embarrassed very easily. The vote is going pretty much the way we anticipated it.

VANOCUR: Wasn't there a drive during the past few days to make sure that people wrote in the name of the President so that the name of the Attorney General would not appear there all alone?

KING: Not really. It is what I recommended.

The results show: Lodge, 33,521 (35.4%); Goldwater, 21,775 (23%); Rockefeller, 19,496 (20.6%); Nixon, 15,752 (16.6%); Smith, 2,812 (3%), Stassen, 1,285 (1.4%). It is an upset victory for Ambassador Lodge. The candidates who campaigned strenuously and spent lavishly are overthrown by a man who is 10,000 miles away, who made not a single speech, shook not a single hand, and whose name was not even on the ballot.

"I goofed up some place," says Sen. Goldwater. Gov. Rockefeller says, "This is a victory for moderation." The winner's backers joyously proclaim, "Ambassador Lodge has emerged as the people's choice."

On Wednesday morning, the very day after the primary, Gov. Rockefeller flies to California to campaign in that all-important contest. Sen. Goldwater rests in Phoenix, but two days later he, too, is campaigning in California.

WISCONSIN

As the Republican contenders wage their battle in California, the Democrats get set for a fight of their own in Wisconsin. Democratic Gov. John Reynolds heads a slate of Wisconsin delegates pledged to

President Johnson. On the Republican side, Rep. John Byrnes runs as a Favorite Son candidate, the result of an agreement between Sen. Goldwater and Gov. Rockefeller to stay out of the Wisconsin race.

But what would have been a lackluster campaign ignites when Alabama's Gov. George Wallace enters the Democratic primary. In his Alabama inaugural address, Gov. Wallace had called for "segregation now, segregation tomorrow, segregation forever!" Now he is ready to invade the North in search of a segregationist following. On March 17, he opens his campaign in Appleton, Wisconsin, home of the late Sen. Joseph McCarthy. What Gov. Wallace says is a forerunner of primaries to come: "The passage of the civil rights bill [being debated in the U. S. Senate] will destroy the system of government in this country." In Oshkosh, he says the bill will make "the President of the United States a total dictator."

Gov. Reynolds urges citizens to "vote for decency" by rejecting Gov. Wallace, whom he calls a "hate monger" who is "deliberately spreading lies." Other Wisconsin Democrats join the battle. Sen. William Proxmire says "a vote for Wallace is a vote for the bigotry that provoked the terrible church bombings that took the lives of four little innocent Negro girls." In Oshkosh, clergymen challenge the Alabaman to differentiate between "segregation" and "racism," and church leaders across the State unite to denounce him. And Sam Hay, acting head of the Goldwater movement in Wisconsin, predicts that many Republicans will cross Party lines to vote for Gov. Wallace. "There are many who feel that civil rights is being badly handled and is going too fast. A vote for Wallace would be their way of protesting," Mr. Hay says. On April 7, Wisconsin primary night, NBC reports on the results.

FLOYD KALBER [in Milwaukee]: There is obvious support here of Gov. Wallace and his attempt to weaken or to destroy the civil rights bill. On the basis of just over half the returns, Wallace can be expected to poll approximately 20 per cent of the total vote. Earlier tonight the Alabama Governor addressed his Wisconsin backers:

WALLACE: I come here tonight to thank you, the people of Wisconsin. I say the work that you have done will do much in both national Parties. It is going to do much in Washington. It is going to let people know that there are more of us who believe in individual liberty and freedom and states' rights than there are those who believe in centralized governmental control over our lives.

KALBER: Gov. Reynolds, concerned about Wallace's spellbinding effect on Wisconsin's ultraconservatives and ethnic groups, campaigned hard. At a news conference earlier he said:

REYNOLDS: I hope we will overwhelm Gov. Wallace. I would hope that his percentage of the vote would be 10 per cent or less. I have not particularly enjoyed this. It has been a weird campaign. I have a feeling that I am running against a man out of the 19th century.

VANOCUR: [To Gov. Reynolds later on]: Gov. Wallace now seems likely to get over 20 per cent of the vote. What is your interpretation of this?

REYNOLDS: One: it means that the Republicans have split their vote between John Byrnes and Gov. Wallace. Two: it means that the people of Wisconsin have vindicated themselves. We have voted four-to-one against Gov. Wallace and what he stands for. The most controversial issue in America today is that civil rights bill, and I think the people of Wisconsin have demonstrated they are willing to support it. The Wallace people spent a terrific amount of money, spreading a lot of falsehoods about the bill. They played upon the fears of the people, and I think the amazing thing is how they only got 20 per cent of the vote.

When the final results are tabulated, they show Gov. Reynolds the winner by a two-to-one margin, but Gov. Wallace has rolled up a vote in Wisconsin far exceeding almost anyone's expectations. The figures: Reynolds, 522,405 (66.2%); Wallace, 266,136 (33.8%). On the Republican side, Rep. Byrnes polled 294,724. The overall vote percentages: Reynolds 47.8%, Byrnes 27.7%, and Wallace 24.5%. Still in Wisconsin, Gov. Wallace says jubilantly the next day: "We won a victory and we know it. We won without winning. Your Governor said if I got 100,000 votes it would be a catastrophe. Well, I guess we've got two catastrophes." Gov. Reynolds counters: "Wallace has lost and lost big." In Washington, where the civil rights bill is before the Senate, Democratic Sen. Hubert Humphrey, floor manager for the bill, says "Gov. Wallace's effort was a flop, f-l-o-p. His campaign was a fizzle, f-i-z-z-l-e." But Republican Sen. Everett McKinley Dirksen is more cautious: "Gov. Wallace's vote is an interesting commentary on the depth of feeling people evidently entertain regarding the civil rights issue."

ILLINOIS ET AL.

On April 9, Gov. Scranton holds a press conference. He says that while he had considered "announcing flatly that even if drafted" he would turn down the Republican nomination, "only the fact that I believe no American has the right to take that position prevents me from so doing." The Governor continues, "But I want those who have been supporting my possible candidacy to clearly understand that from this day forward I cannot be held accountable for encouraging their efforts in the slightest degree. The only thing I have not ruled out is a draft."

Tuesday, April 14, is the day of the Illinois primary. Since the Illinois vote is not binding on the delegates, many consider it merely a popularity contest. Sen. Goldwater has one opponent on the ballot, Sen. Margaret Chase Smith. On primary night, Frank McGee sums up from Chicago.

McGEE: Sen. Goldwater made only three campaign appearances in Illinois—one last November, another in February, and the third last weekend. At a "Youth for Goldwater" rally in Chicago the Senator's target was President Johnson.

GOLDWATER: We now have a President who tries to save money by turning off lights in the White House even as he heads towards a staggering addition to our national debt. Somebody has suggested that LBJ should stand for "Light Bulb" Johnson, and we can turn him off in 1964.

McGEE: Sen. Margaret Chase Smith has been in Illinois only twice. Her campaign has been a lean one—little or no money, no paid workers, no purchase of radio or TV time, no newspaper ads. Two days ago, at a Chicago news conference, she was asked why she had picked the Illinois primary.

SEN. SMITH: I think the people have a right to have a second choice. I don't understand why all of the candidates aren't in here. I would like to see all candidates declare themselves and get into the primaries and show the people what they stand for.

McGEE: The Illinois Presidential primary today was intended to prove the obvious—that conservative Sen. Goldwater was the odds-on choice of this State's Republicans, who are largely conservative. But it has not really done that. Goldwater has won the Presidential primary, but not as overwhelmingly as local experts had said he must to overcome his defeat in New Hampshire. As they saw it, Goldwater would have to get 80 per cent of the votes cast. Sen. Smith said she would be happy with 10 per cent of the Illinois vote. Promoters of Henry Cabot Lodge and Richard Nixon asked voters not to write their names on the ballot — either because they thought Goldwater had it anyway, or because of the difficulty of writing in names when voting machines are used.

The co-chairmen of the Illinois "Goldwater for President" committee said tonight they were not surprised that Sen. Smith made a strong showing against their man. Here is Congressman Edward Derwinski, a Goldwater leader. To what do you attribute Mrs. Smith's strong showing?

DERWINSKI: To the people who were interested in Romney, Scranton, Nixon, Lodge or Stassen, a vote for Mrs. Smith was, in effect, a vote for their own candidate. I interpret it as the rest of the field versus Goldwater by means of Mrs. Smith.

The official Illinois totals give Sen. Goldwater 512,-840, which is just under 47% of the Republican vote cast. In the gubernatorial race, Charles Percy, a Republican moderate, trounces William Scott, a Goldwater supporter. The final Presidential tally: Goldwater, 512,840; Smith, 209,521; Lodge, 68,122; Nixon, 30,313; Wallace, 2,203; Rockefeller, 2,048; Scranton, 1,842; Romney, 465.

Back in the White House, President Lyndon B. Johnson tells a press conference on April 18, "I will stay out" of the political arena "as long as I can." Two days later he offers to provide intelligence briefings to "major" candidates. Sen. Goldwater rejects the proposal, calling it "less than wise and less than wholehearted." Gov. Rockefeller accepts, but says, "I reserve the right to continue to comment." During the next two weeks, the President delivers more than two dozen speeches; holds three press conferences; announces the settlement of the railroad dispute on network television; tours the Appalachia poverty area and talks to Kentucky miners; meets with the President of Venezuela; dedicates a cultural center to President Kennedy; orders a reappraisal of the draft; visits Pittsburgh, Atlantic City, Chicago and South Bend; flies to the New York World's Fair for a civil rights speech; meets with religious

leaders; hosts a White House dinner for labor leaders, confers with historians; addresses the U.S. Chamber of Commerce, and is photographed picking up his beagles by the ears. At one of his press conferences, the President is asked if he thinks "overexposure" to the public could be a problem for him. The President answers: "Well, I strive to please...and I hope the press will never be critical of me for being over-accessible." Answering another question, the President tells the newsmen: "I don't have any aches and pains. I feel fine. I get adequate rest, good pay, and plenty to eat. And I don't know of anyone that's concerned about my health."

Meanwhile, Republican primaries are coming one after another. On April 28, Gov. Scranton sets a new Pennsylvania record, with 220,573 write-in votes on a primary ballot that does not list Presidential candidates. Far behind are Lodge (79,781); Nixon (36,686); Goldwater (32,305); and Rockefeller (7,160).

On May 1, Georgia Republicans gather in Atlanta for their State convention. Robert MacNeil reports.

MacNEIL: Georgia was one of the few Southern States in which Goldwater felt it necessary to woo delegates in person. It was necessary because it threatened to crack his solid Southern phalanx. Although he already had 18 of the State's 24 delegates, Goldwater flew all the way back from California to the Georgia convention to win the other six. He got four of them in the twenty-four hour visit, but psychologically, it was one of the lowest points of his campaign. He was exhausted by travel, and irritated by thrusting microphones and the increasing number of newsmen. Arriving late at night in Atlanta, the Senator woke up to find an unscheduled crowd of friends at the airport. He got annoyed, wanted to know who was responsible for arranging a demonstration and refused to leave the plane. Finally, campaign director Denison Kitchel went back to him and said, "Dammit, Barry, you're a national figure." Reluctantly, the national figure got out of the plane and suffered himself to be adored. But he was in good humor by the time he got to the convention itself.

On May 2, Texas holds its first Presidential primary ever. The Texas primary has no standing in law, and is merely a popularity contest sponsored by the pro-Goldwater Republican State Committee. When

Gov. Rockefeller's name is placed on the ballot over his protests, he says: "I don't think it's a primary; I think it's a stacked deck and a rigged deal." Sen. Goldwater wins the election, piling up 100,909 votes to 23,552 for Lodge, Rockefeller and Nixon combined.

Although Sen. Goldwater is the only candidate on the Nebraska primary ballot of May 12, he gets only 49.5% of the vote. An intensive write-in campaign for Richard Nixon gives the former Vice President 31.5%, and Ambassador Lodge receives 16.2%. That same day, Gov. Rockefeller sweeps to a 100% victory in West Virginia: he is the only candidate on the ballot and no write-ins are permitted.

As for the Democrats, the Indiana primary on May 5 is Gov. Wallace's second venture into a Northern contest. And again a Democratic governor (this time, Indiana's Gov. Matthew Welsh) represents President Johnson on the ballot. On the Republican side, Sen. Goldwater faces only token opposition in Harold Stassen. Also on the Indiana ballot are Lar Daly, who campaigns in an Uncle Sam costume, and Mrs. Fay T. Carpenter-Swain, who says she wants "everything free." On primary night, Frank McGee reports from Indianapolis.

McGEE: Indiana's Gov. Matthew Welsh, stand-in for President Johnson, has won this State's Democratic primary, beating back a determined drive by Alabama's fiery segregationist, Gov. George Wallace. But Wallace—by taking about 30 per cent of the vote—claims he has shaken the liberals in both parties. Wallace's showing here has been almost exactly the same as it was a month ago in the Wisconsin primary.

WALLACE: When we first came here, the pollsters and the liberals said we would not get any such vote as we have gotten. The campaign was very vigorous against us. In my judgment, this is indicative of the fact that there are millions of people in this country who are very concerned at trends in our government. I also want to say I do not consider that this vote is against any segment of our population. I do not believe that people voting for me were voting against anyone. They were voting against some of the methods that are being used to solve the problems that face the American people.

McGEE: The Indiana Democratic organization campaigned on the slogan, "Clear the way for LBJ,

vote for Welsh on the fifth of May." Here is how the Governor viewed the outcome:

WELSH: This cannot properly be called a Wallace victory. We had a massive cross-over of Republicans voting in the Democratic primary.

Gov. Welsh holds the State for President Johnson with 376,023 votes (65%). Gov. Wallace gets 172,646 (29.8%). Mr. Daly gets 15,160 votes (2.6%), and Mrs. Carpenter-Swain receives 7,140 votes (1.2%). On the Republican side, Sen. Goldwater overwhelms Mr. Stassen, 267,935 to 107,157—67% to 26.8%.

"We shook the eye-teeth of those people in Wisconsin," says Gov. Wallace, "and the noises you hear now are the teeth falling out in Indiana. We're going on to Maryland from here."

The Alabama Governor is to make his strongest showing in his third and final primary: Maryland, on May 19. Here, President Johnson's stand-in is Sen. Daniel Brewster. The Senator wins as Maryland Democrats vote in record numbers, but Gov. Wallace takes 16 counties to the Senator's seven. The Maryland vote is 267,104 for Sen. Brewster to 214,837 for the Alabama Governor. "Everyone knows we won a victory here tonight," Gov. Wallace says. "We have a majority of the white vote. If the Republicans could have crossed over, we'd have beaten the hell out of them, sure enough." Sen. Brewster responds: "There is no substitute for victory," and he notes with satisfaction that at the Democratic Convention, Maryland's votes will go to President Johnson.

OREGON

The climactic Republican primary fights take place on the Pacific Coast. There, attention focuses first on the battle for the 18 delegates from Oregon. On the eve of the May 15 Oregon primary, NBC News reports.

McGEE: The Oregon primary is different. In the others, the candidates decide if they will run; in this one, the people decide — at least indirectly. Oregon's Secretary of State enters the names of the candidates most people are talking about for the Presidency. As a result, this is the first time the names of six candidates have been printed on the ballot, giving the voters a full choice.

Oregon is important to each contender, but for different reasons. Two of them—Gov. Scranton and Mrs. Smith—know they have no prospect of winning this primary. No one has campaigned here for them. Two others have not campaigned in person because they find it is better politics at the moment to claim they are not candidates: Ambassador Lodge and former Vice President Nixon. The remaining two candidates have campaigned in Oregon: Sen. Goldwater and Gov. Rockefeller. Both were hurt badly when they lost in New Hampshire to Lodge. All the polls show that Lodge will win this one also. Rockefeller's strategy calls for a handsome win over Goldwater in Oregon to help him in California, where their names are the only ones on the ballot. Oregon offers Ambassador Lodge the last chance to prove he has public support and pick up delegates to the Convention. What he earned in New Hampshire and may earn here will be almost all the real strength he could take to the Convention.

VANOCUR: Henry Cabot Lodge, the absentee candidate, is carrying on his work as Ambassador in Saigon. Despite his impressive victory in the New Hampshire primary, Lodge has made no effort to return home to campaign—a decision which reflects his assessment that his best strategy is to stay on the job in South Vietnam. In his absence, his work is being carried on by his son, George, and volunteers working in his behalf.

McGEE: Oregon will send only 18 delegates to the Convention. California will send 86. A few weeks ago, Sen. Goldwater cancelled all further personal campaigning in Oregon. Reporting on this development is NBC's Robert MacNeil.

MacNEIL: Barry Goldwater believes that the primaries are not the important part of getting nominated. So far, he has been proving it. He loses primaries but he is piling up delegates elsewhere. In this process, Oregon is almost irrelevant to him, but not quite. The issues that betrayed him in New Hampshire came back to haunt him here. Would he hurt Social Security? Would he cause war? Vigorously, his organization refuted these themes. The machinery ground on, but so did the adverse

polls. Money was short and so was time. The really crucial prize of California's 86 delegates glittered to the South. But Goldwater could not afford a bald retreat. It had to be a tactful as well as a tactical withdrawal. He found the means in the civil rights bill and, pleading duty, he suddenly cancelled all his remaining appearances. Still, the campaign could not simply be dismantled. The stunned Oregon workers had to convince themselves he had not written them off.

So, reinforcements came. Barry, Jr., an effective younger version of the Senator from jaw line to philosophy, campaigned hard to fight the Rockefeller line that Goldwater did not care enough to come back. Gen. Albert Wedemeyer, World War II Asia expert, came out to speak. The aim was to prevent a defeat so colossal that it would have a bad psychological effect on California.

McGEE: The primaries are not important to former Vice President Nixon. His best chance for the nomination lies in a deadlock between the conservative forces of Sen. Goldwater and the moderate or liberal forces represented by all the other candidates. Nixon is keeping himself in circulation. Shortly after Ambassador Lodge won the New Hampshire primary, Nixon took off on a tour of Southeast Asia that included a stop at Lodge's post in Saigon. The tour and his speeches helped to keep Nixon's name alive. Just a couple of days after Nixon's return, some of his supporters in Oregon opened a campaign headquarters for him.

BRINKLEY: We are seeing here an unusual political campaign: six candidates, five of them absent — as though they were trying to run a beauty contest without girls. Rockefeller is doing himself some good by being here, but three of the others — Goldwater, Lodge and Nixon — are trying to win it without showing their faces. Some of their devices are interesting, possibly effective.

Lodge is trying to win it by mail order. His people are mailing cards to registered Republicans asking for pledges. And when they come back, the information is put on five-part carbon paper forms. Well, this makes for a lot of paper shuffling and it is, therefore, the kind of job that could be automated, with each voter becoming a set of holes in a punch card. We may all come to that.

Sen. Goldwater, who is not here either, is having his campaigning done for him by family and friends. They are holding rallies, making speeches and saying the things Goldwater would say if he were here. Families, of course, have been used in primaries before, but usually with the candidate and not in place of him. So that is new.

And Nixon has had fifty telephones installed upstairs out of sight, and hired fifty girls to call around drumming up votes for him. This was kept secret until NBC got pictures of it the other night. They told us then that they were taking a poll for some kind of magazine. Perhaps: "would the readers like more recipes or more fashions?" But now that it is out, they are saying their telephone girls find surprising support for Nixon. And, in the meantime, Rockefeller is himself out shaking hands, making speeches and doing it in the old fashioned way. So we have four kinds of campaigning — by mail, by telephone, by proxy, and in person. Friday night, we will find out the winning candidate and the winning system.

F*air weather covers Oregon on Friday, May 15, and the voters — aware that the eyes of the nation are upon them — go to the polls in large numbers. The result is a surprise victory for Gov. Rockefeller in the State. Ambassador Lodge, the predicted winner, is second, and Sen. Goldwater, third — just 2,163 votes ahead of Richard Nixon. The totals: Rockefeller, 93,032 (33%); Lodge, 78,227 (27.7%); Goldwater, 49,784 (17.6%); Nixon, 47,621 (16.8%); Smith, 8,268 (2.9%); and Scranton, 5,716 (2%). Paul Grindle, national director of the "Draft Lodge" movement, concedes victory to Gov. Rockefeller an hour after the polls close. He says: "There is not the slightest question that Oregon voters have seen one of the greatest finishes in political history. They have seen an incredible fighter with lots of guts, who has gone on slugging since New Hampshire. I think the Oregon voters have gone along with us in expressing their admiration for Nelson A. Rockefeller." In Los Angeles, Sen. Goldwater says: "I still have 325 delegates. I am glad he [Gov. Rockefeller] has some — it makes a better race."*

CALIFORNIA

This is the last contested State primary prior to the Republican Convention. Ever since New Hampshire, Sen. Goldwater has said that if he is to be the Republican nominee, he must win in California. The battle between the Senator and Gov. Rockefeller is joined. The prize is 86 California delegates. One week before the June 2 California primary, an important Republican voice is heard. Gen. Eisenhower writes a statement for the NEW YORK HERALD TRIBUNE describing the type of candidate he hopes the Republicans will nominate. It is generally agreed that his specifications fit every candidate except Sen. Goldwater. In a lighthearted mood, the Senator poses for a photograph with an arrow seemingly stuck in his back. He says the picture typifies "some of the problems I've had in the last few days." But in a formal statement, he says, "I endorse Gen. Eisenhower's excellent statement...I hail its forthright restatement of the basic Republican principles upon which I proudly stand." Questioned in Washington by a reporter who wants to know if Sen. Goldwater fits the statement's specifications, Gen. Eisenhower replies, "try to fit that shoe on that foot."

On the Saturday preceding the primary, a son is born to the Rockefellers, thus focusing attention anew on the New York Governor's divorce and remarriage.

Two days before the California primary, NBC assesses the two candidates' positions.

McGEE: A California Republican in this primary is like a housewife compelled to choose between two bruised apples. She doesn't really want either of them, but she must take one if she's to have any apple at all. Over half the Republicans here don't want to vote for either Sen. Barry Goldwater or Gov. Nelson Rockefeller as their Party's Presidential nominee. But they must if they vote, because only their names are on the ballot and no other can be written in.

Rockefeller's prospects in California, very dim not many weeks ago, brightened dramatically by his upset victory in Oregon. That contest prompted a move by the Lodge forces.

A LODGE SUPPORTER: We will work to mobilize the substantial Lodge support in California and then we'll ask these Lodge supporters to vote for Gov. Rockefeller's delegate slate in the California primary. By doing this, we will be increasing Ambassador Lodge's eventual delegate support at the national Convention in San Francisco. We are not leading a "Stop Goldwater" movement. We are working to secure the nomination of Ambassador Lodge.

GOLDWATER: It's a "Stop Goldwater" movement. That's all it is and we'll treat it as such.

ROCKEFELLER: No deals have been made. It's a pro-Lodge move, as far as they're concerned. I'm interested in a pro-Rockefeller move and delighted to have votes from the Lodge supporters.

McGEE: In the campaign, Rockefeller has been on the attack, trying to turn Goldwater's own remarks against him. Goldwater, who no longer speaks off the cuff, has been on the defensive, trying to temper his earlier statements and rid himself of the stigma of extremism.

ROCKEFELLER: As a person, I like Barry Goldwater, but I deeply disagree with him on some of the fundamental issues facing our country today. Sen. Goldwater said he wants to see Social Security made voluntary. You and I know that would bankrupt the system and undermine the security of the fifteen million Americans who presently have these benefits as their platform of security in their old age.

GOLDWATER: If we add to the cost of Social Security, which by 1970 will be roughly 10 per cent [of the payroll] divided between the employee and employer; if we add to this the cost of medicare, which many propose (I don't); then if we do as some people are advocating, tack on the cost of a nationwide mental health plan, I can see this share between the employer and employee reaching possibly 25 or 30 per cent.

ROCKEFELLER: Sen. Goldwater said he would have us pull out of the United Nations and specifically mentioned that in relation to Red China if Red China is admitted. I'm opposed to the admission of Red China, but utterly opposed to our pulling out of the United Nations.

GOLDWATER: The United Nations in some situations can mediate disputes. It can often provide

a useful forum for the airing of differences. But there can be—either in the United Nations or in the councils of the free world—no substitute for the leadership of the United States. And one other important point: the United Nations cannot make policy for the United States.

ROCKEFELLER: One of the issues is whether the extreme Right will take over the Party and pull the Party out of the mainstream of American thought and away from responsible Republicanism.

GOLDWATER: You people, who are fired up, are concerned about the course our country is engaged in. Not that you're extremists; not that you're afraid. But you are exercising the rightful prerogative of every American—whether he's Democrat, Republican or nonpartisan — and that prerogative is to express yourselves at the polls in the way that you feel is best for your country. And don't let any politician scare you out of it.

MacNEIL: In the dying moments of this campaign, Barry Goldwater has almost become the professionally managed candidate that he's scorned for months. One of the most quixotic men in politics, Goldwater genuinely believed that he could campaign by being candid about his views and not attacking his opponents. He thought these were his strong points. Both got him in trouble and have been finally abandoned. His candor revealed a habit of improvising positions on key issues that left doubt in many minds. Rockefeller exploited these doubts; forced Goldwater to spend months on the defensive. He entered this final stretch in California devoting all his energy to proving he wasn't an extremist, war monger or wrecker of Social Security. Finally, this past week he turned to a spirited attack on Rockefeller himself. To the end, he has remained a leisurely, confident, though more disciplined campaigner.

On June 1, the eve of the California primary, Gen. Eisenhower denies that his recent statement describing the ideal Republican candidate was anti-Goldwater. To read that into the statement, he says, is a "complete misinterpretation." "I never attempted to read anyone out of the Party."

On June 2, the voters in America's most populous State go to the polls. Soon after the first returns are in that night, Frank McGee reports from Los Angeles.

McGEE: What the seasoned political observers seemed to sense through their pores is so far holding true. It is a very, very tight race—the closest race we have had this year.

MacNEIL [from Goldwater headquarters]: The Senator's supporters have the scent of victory in their nostrils. The Senator himself spent this very crucial day in his life in an impressive display of casualness, going shopping and having his hair cut, while his staff grew more and more excited about last minute polls putting him nearer and nearer to Rockefeller. The Senator himself plans to hear the result here in California, then fly back to Washington in mid-evening.

HUNTLEY: This contest has been, of course, a political popularity contest between two men—but it also featured an almost classic confrontation between the progressive Republicanism of Rockefeller and the conservatism of Goldwater. Yet, it has been still a third thing—a process to determine the course of the Republican party in this State for perhaps the next ten years. Those who were ideologically in sympathy with the New York Governor had no hesitation in declaring that a Goldwater win here today would put the Party out of business for the next ten years. They declared that the Democrats in November would overwhelm the candidates identified with Goldwater.

Goldwater candidates, on the other hand, seemed less concerned about November and more intent on today's contest. They declared that the time had come for the GOP to undertake a change, and the Senator was the man to do it. Thus, a Goldwater victory here today would mean changes in the Party, changes in leadership, changes in candidates and office holders and, to some extent, a change in philosophy.

BRINKLEY: Whatever happens tonight in California, the primaries and spring formals and the junior proms are over. In the months since New Hampshire, Republicans in the primary States

have been asked to decide between a choice and an echo and each time until tonight, perhaps, they have chosen the echo. But when the Convention opens in San Francisco next month, they will not be looking for echoes or slogans or any cute phrases from campaign posters. They will be looking for a winner; that is, somebody who can beat Lyndon Johnson. No Republican willing to be honest thinks it will be easy and some of them in their private moments think it will be impossible. But the election is still six months away.

Anyway, the primaries began in New Hampshire on snow shoes and ended in Los Angeles under the palm trees. And some of their more memorable sights included Pierre Salinger making a speech on a tennis court in Beverly Hills while a girl stood off to one side holding his cigar; a woman coming to a shopping center in Oregon to hear Rockefeller speak and saying to a reporter, "I'm not going to vote for him. I just came to see what Happy saw in him;" George Lodge flying 3,000 miles to Oregon and mounting a political platform to announce he was taking no part in his father's campaign; and an excursion boat filled with Goldwater boosters sailing outward from Los Angeles through shark infested waters to Catalina Island to hear him speak and, on the way, singing the best campaign song to appear so far, "Hello, Dolly," rewritten with a new set of words beginning, "Hello, Barry."

It has been a gaudy time. We could, of course, choose our leaders as, say, the British do in elections that are free, quiet and cheap — where the speeches are not very extravagant, the poster is not very big, the music not very good (if there is any), and where nobody spends much money even if he has it. Rockefeller alone must have spent enough to buy a Polaris submarine or maybe to wipe out at least one pocket of poverty. But now it is over until the Convention, when the Democrats nominate Lyndon Johnson and the Republicans nominate somebody they hope can beat him. As yet, in spite of all the primaries and all the money, nobody is sure who that will be.

All night long, as the vote pours in, Sen. Goldwater clings to a precarious lead. It is so close that even after midnight, Gov. Rockefeller, in New York, refuses to concede. He congratulates the Senator on "the tremendous number of votes he is rolling up," but insists that "the show isn't over." In Los Angeles, when it appears evident to Sen. Goldwater he will win, the Senator says, "This is not a victory for Barry Goldwater. It's a victory for the mainstream of Republican thinking." He also predicts "a greater and greater 'Stop Goldwater' movement. I do not have this thing sewed up. We have a ways to go." He adds that his victory is "a giant step" towards the nomination.

The final California vote gives Sen. Goldwater 1,089,133, for 51.4%, and Gov. Rockefeller 1,030,180, for 48.6%. Out of 2,119,313 votes cast, the Senator wins by 58,953. This is the only primary Sen. Goldwater has won in which he has had real competition. And because of California's 86 delegate votes and the Goldwater victory's enormous psychological impact, this final Republican primary provides the most important political victory of the year so far.

THE AFTERMATH

The 40 days between the California primary and the Republican Convention are filled with a drama seldom matched in American political history.

With Gov. Rockefeller defeated in California, the moderates turn to Gov. William Scranton of Pennsylvania. But the Governor disappoints them when, in a Harrisburg press conference, he says he knows of no "basic differences" between Sen. Goldwater and himself, and asserts that he won't try to prevent the Senator's nomination. That assertion appears temporary, however, for on Saturday, June 6, Gov. Scranton goes to Gettysburg at Gen. Eisenhower's invitation, where the two men confer alone for 85 minutes. Gen. Eisenhower asks the Governor to relax

his demand for an "honest draft," and Gov. Scranton agrees to be available for the Republican Presidential nomination if the delegates want him.

On Sunday morning, June 7, Gov. Scranton flies to the annual Governors' Conference in Cleveland, where he is to make a nationwide television appearance. The Governor carries with him a written statement that will clearly indicate his availability for the nomination. But shortly before he goes on the air, Gen. Eisenhower telephones him to say that the Governor has misunderstood their Gettysburg meeting and that the General will refuse to participate in any "Stop Goldwater" movement. Gov. Scranton goes ahead with his TV appearance but does not read his statement. After the broadcast Gov. Rockefeller publicly ridicules Gov. Scranton's indecisiveness. Meanwhile, former Vice President Nixon declares that Sen. Goldwater's philosophy must be "challenged and repudiated."

BRINKLEY [June 11]: Gen. Eisenhower says again that he is not trying to stop Goldwater or anyone else. He says he is plain disgusted at all the reports saying he is. In Gettysburg today he said he was angry about the reports that he tried to push Gov. Scranton into the race and then telephoned him the next day and tried to pull him back out. The General said he did ask Scranton to make himself more available, and did telephone him the next day and say that he didn't mean he was trying to push him into being a candidate. But he insists that he is not trying to stop Goldwater.

That night—June 11—Gov. Scranton changes his mind again. He decides to run and immediately accepts a long-standing invitation to address the Maryland Republican Convention in Baltimore the next day.

HIGHLIGHTS FROM GOV. SCRANTON'S ADDRESS

Can we pretend, even to ourselves, that it is possible for us to stand with one foot in the 20th Century and the other in the 19th? We have no right to sell out to the modern expediences of the easy answer, or the fast draw, or the quick solution. I say that the true spirit of the Republican Party today stands equally dedicated to preserving this nation from the dry rot of phony liberalism or the slow death of blind reaction. Let us be

done with the fear spread by the small-minded in our own Party who hint that America has not enough prosperity to go all the way around . . . Lincoln would cry out in pain if we sold out on our principles—but he would laugh out with scorn if we threw away an election.

I've come here to offer our Party a real choice. I reject the echo we have thus far been handed — the echo of fear and of reaction, the echo of the never-never land that puts our nation on the road backward to a lesser place in the world of free men. I come here to announce that I am a candidate for the Presidency of the United States.

BRINKLEY [at the Lord Baltimore Hotel]: Several times Goldwater people booed him. At some of his cutting references, they were seen to put their hands to their heads in expressions of pain and incredulity. His speech was short, cool, cutting — and very much to the point. His point being that the Republican Party and its candidates for local, State and Federal offices need to be saved from disaster. He said all that without ever mentioning Sen. Goldwater by name. After his speech, Gov. Scranton said that his decision was made so suddenly that he doesn't even have a campaign manager, a speaking itinerary, or other standard appurtenances of a candidate for President.

VANOCUR: Gov. William Scranton became a candidate because he was angry. He was angry at Sen. Goldwater for voting against ending the filibuster in the civil rights debate. He was angry at what he thought was Gen. Eisenhower's urging him last weekend to get into the race, and then pulling out the rug from under him the next day. He was angry about the humiliation he felt at the Governors' Conference in Cleveland when Rockefeller and others expressed public scorn about his refusal to enter the race and, perhaps most important of all, he was angry when he heard that one member of his staff—who expressed concern to a Goldwater supporter about what a Goldwater candidacy would do to local tickets in Pennsylvania—was told by the Goldwater man: "We've

already written off Pennsylvania." Yesterday, he sat down with his family, his aides, and other close political associates, and made his decision.

The bitterness of Gov. Scranton's remarks sting Sen. Goldwater, who is interviewed in Washington shortly after by Peter Hackes. "The Republican Establishment is desperate to defeat me," the Senator says. "They can't stand having someone they can't control." He charges that Mr. Nixon is behind Gov. Scranton's entry into the race. "It's just like Nixon to set this up and then run off to London, as he's done." But other Republicans welcome Gov. Scranton into the race. Governors Rockefeller and Romney say they're glad he has joined the battle. Gen. Eisenhower calls the candidacy good for the health and vigor of the Party. Richard Nixon, in London, says: "Gov. Scranton's entry is a healthy thing for the Party—but I, under no circumstance, will endorse him or anybody else before the Convention." While praise is plentiful, only the supporters of Henry Cabot Lodge speak specifically of giving Gov. Scranton their votes.

Gov. Scranton continues his barrage on a criss-cross tour of the nation in a last-minute search for delegates. He gets a lift on Thursday, when Milton Eisenhower announces he will nominate the Governor in San Francisco. But while the Governor spends the week searching for votes, Sen. Goldwater spends it getting the votes. He wins all 56 delegates in Texas, and all 14 in Montana. In Texas, the Senator sounds a note that is a forerunner of things to come. "Radical columnists and newspapers," he tells the Texans, "are very concerned about what happens to the Republican Party. Nothing could make them happier than if the Republican Party would drown."

As the battle continues, a vote by the Senate in Washington, D.C., marks a turning point in the nation's history. A year before, President John F. Kennedy had sent his civil rights message to the Congress. "It is time to act," he warned. Now, on Friday, June 19—one year later to the very day—every member of the United States Senate is in his seat, ready to act on the civil rights bill. The roll call begins at 7:40 pm, and a few minutes later, the bill passes the Senate, 73 to 27. Only six Senate Republicans vote against it—and one of them is Sen. Goldwater, who charges that parts of the bill are unconstitutional. Sen. Dirksen, Republican Senate leader, votes in the affirmative, and President Johnson proclaims that it is "a challenge to men of good will ... to transform the commands of our law into the customs of our land." Next step for the bill is the House of Representatives.

Gov. Scranton wires Sen. Goldwater and says his vote against civil rights was contrary to the traditional Republican philosophy of equal opportunity for all. Goldwater answers by accusing Scranton of asking him to sell out his principles. The Senator says he believes in equal rights as firmly as anyone, but he does not believe in threatening the rights and liberties of all the people.

On June 23, Ambassador Henry Cabot Lodge announces his resignation, saying he will return to the United States to aid Gov. Scranton. The Ambassador expresses the hope that Vietnam will not become a campaign issue.

Sen. Goldwater retorts by saying he hopes Lodge will not become "a lone Republican voice crying excuses about the Administration's policy." And he rebukes the Ambassador for leaving his post "at such a critical time." Gov. Scranton welcomes the Lodge support, but says that "as far as I'm concerned, Vietnam is still an issue."

On June 29, Gov. Scranton, en route to Miami in quest of delegates, says flatly, "Goldwater can't win (against President Johnson)." It is the first time he has publicly expressed this theme in a pre-Convention campaign that is turning up little delegate support.

VANOCUR: Gov. Scranton and his staff decided this weekend that he would have to intensify his efforts to provoke Sen. Goldwater into some kind of response. Despite what he says publicly, Scranton knows he has not been making any important headway with delegates, and he decided to do something dramatic. From Atlanta, where he is seeking delegates, he wired Sen. Goldwater challenging him to debate the issue in Chicago tomorrow, before a meeting of the Illinois delegation.

Sen. Goldwater accepts the challenge, and on June 30 he, Gov. Scranton and Harold Stassen speak before the Illinois delegation—with 58 votes at stake. After the speeches, a tally shows 48 for the Senator, five leaning toward him, and five uncommitted. Gov. Scranton does not receive a single vote. Vanocur reports: "Gov. Scranton's candidacy reached its anticlimax in Illinois today." The coup de grace is administered by Sen. Dirksen, who announces that, if asked, he will personally nominate Sen. Goldwater at San Francisco.

Meanwhile, on July 2, David Brinkley reports on the progress of the civil rights bill through the House.

BRINKLEY: Congress passed the civil rights bill today. There's been more than a year of oratory, argument and filibuster, leaving not much more to say about it. The House voted 289 to 126 to

accept the amendments made in the Senate. The last words spoken in Congress before the final vote came from Rep. Emanuel Celler of New York: "Let there be no more arguments and no more speeches. The country demands action, and action is eloquent. Let us vote to redeem the American pledge of equal opportunity for all."

*L*ater in the day—in a nationally televised ceremony — President Johnson signs the bill in the presence of leaders of both Parties. Sen. Goldwater lets it be known that he is afraid of a violent civil rights explosion this summer and asks church, Negro and other leaders for advice on how to avoid it.

The battle for the Republican Presidential nomination moves toward its climax during the week before the Republican Convention. In San Francisco, the 100-member Platform Committee, heavily weighted with Goldwater supporters, holds hearings on the political issues.

BRINKLEY: The problem is how to write a statement on the civil rights bill, and then to nominate a candidate who voted against it in the Senate. The Scranton forces want to say the bill is constitutional, while the Goldwater people think it is not. The Scranton strategy is to try to force some kind of showdown in the Platform Committee, and if he can't settle it there, to force it out to the Convention floor next week.

Goldwater, on the other hand, is relaxed, serene and secure, as a candidate is only when he has more delegates than he needs. His strategy is to lie low and stay out of sight.

*I*n Illinois, Gov. Scranton embarks on a two-day whistle-stop tour in a vain effort to overturn the decision by that State's delegation to support Sen. Goldwater.

PETTIT: Scranton is campaigning here as if he really believes he can stop Goldwater. He is trying to persuade rank and file Republicans to put pressure on the Goldwater delegation from Illinois. He is using massive television and a whistle-stop train trip. But no matter what he does here, Illinois' Sen. Everett McKinley Dirksen has spoken. And the words he spoke were "Barry Goldwater."

45

CAPTIONS

THE REPUBLICAN CONVENTION

On Wednesday, July 8, the Governor opens his campaign from the scene of the Convention itself. He flies to San Francisco and addresses a large and noisily enthusiastic throng of supporters who come to meet him at the airport.

SCRANTON: I'm here to prove that we are responsible Americans—not radical extremists. And I'm here because we do believe in equal rights for all Americans. [Cheers] And we are not in favor of scuttling the United Nations. [Cheers] And we do not advocate irresponsible use of nuclear weapons. [Cheers] And we want the American people to know that Republicans have seen the calendar and they know that it's 1964, not 1864. [Cheers]

HUNTLEY: The atmosphere here in San Francisco picked up noticeably when Gov. Scranton arrived in town. He certainly was given a surprisingly large reception at the airport and certainly around the Mark Hopkins Hotel.

The climate will be further enlivened again tomorrow when Sen. Goldwater is due to arrive. So, over the weekend, we should have some interest and considerable shows of enthusiasm around the city of San Francisco.

MacNEIL [from Washington]: Barry Goldwater is in his Washington apartment, keeping in constant touch with his staff in San Francisco. The fruitful work of the past six months is over. The delegates have been identified, wooed and collected into a mass solid enough, they feel, to give it to Goldwater on the first ballot.

He has been looking calmly at efforts to flush him out into a fight. By telephone, he's been urging his top staff members in San Francisco not to get excited. He's going to San Francisco tomorrow, determined not to fight with anyone. He believes he's unstoppable, but he'll be the last person to risk crowing about it.

Sen. Goldwater arrives in San Francisco on Thursday, July 9, to a tumultuous airport reception. At a news conference, he offers the opinion that Gov. Scran-

ton would not be willing to be the Vice Presidential nominee because the Governor has called him "ignorant, cowardly, backward, impulsive, and a shooter-from-the-hipper." Meanwhile, in downtown San Francisco, Gov. Scranton appears before the Platform Committee and reminds his listeners that Sen. Goldwater has called Party platforms "a packet of lies and misinformation." On Friday, Sen. Goldwater makes his own appearance before the Platform Committee, and is interrupted by cheers and applause 41 times. The Senator says he is not really concerned with details of the platform, but that if he cannot honestly run on the platform that the Convention finally adopts, he will withdraw from the race. Told of the Goldwater remarks, Scranton snaps, "I don't believe a word of it." One basic conflict facing the Republican Platform Committee is analyzed by Chet Huntley.

HUNTLEY: There is a question, mute and ominous, hovering about this Convention. It licks spasmodically at the proceedings here like the fog which sometimes slips over the Golden Gate and invades the city. In its worst aspects, it may be called racism. Otherwise, it is called the civil rights issue. There are overtones of it in the testimony and the arguments in the Platform Committee.

No one is challenging Sen. Goldwater's assertion that he will have strength in the South. And the California primary revealed that he has strength in the North. Many of his champions argue that there was a strong element of civil rights backlash in his California victory. If this be true, and if Sen. Goldwater is the nominee, then this question is posed: how can the Republican Party take advantage of its opportunity in the South, and exploit the civil rights backlash in the North, without becoming the Party of resistance to the civil rights laws and movements?

By suggestion, that question nags at this Convention, and all the careful words in the platform may not completely disguise it.

O*n Sunday, July 12, the Platform Committee releases its recommendations. The platform attacks the Johnson administration from top to bottom, asserting that it shows "weakness before communism," is run by "Federal extremists," and toys with the "aspirations of minority groups." Moderates call it a*

"Goldwater platform." The Senator's backers call it a "Republican platform."

But the bombshell comes Sunday evening, when Gov. Scranton challenges Sen. Goldwater to a face-to-face confrontation on the floor of the Convention. The challenge is delivered in a letter so scathing that it becomes one of the major issues of the Convention.

TEXT OF GOV. SCRANTON'S LETTER

Dear Senator: As we move rapidly toward the climax of this Convention, the Republican Party faces continuing struggle on two counts. The first involves, of course, selection of a candidate. Here the issue is extremely clear. It's simply this: Will the Convention choose the candidate overwhelmingly favored by the Republican voters, or will it choose you? Your organization does not even argue the merits of the question. They admit that you are a minority candidate, but they feel they have bought, beaten and compromised enough delegate support to make the result a foregone conclusion. With open contempt for the dignity and integrity and common sense of the Convention, your managers say in effect that the delegates are little more than a flock of chickens whose necks will be wrung at will.

I have double-checked the arithmetic of my staff, and I am convinced that a true count at this minute puts your first ballot strength at only some 620 votes. Our count differs from that of your managers because we have calculated an important element which they are incapable of comprehending. That is the element of respect for the men and women who make up the delegations to this Convention. We are not taking them for granted. We are not insulting their intelligence or their integrity. We're not counting noses, we're counting hearts. We're not issuing orders, we're providing a rallying point for responsibility in the Republican Party.

You will be stopped on the first ballot because a sufficient number of your nominal supporters have already indicated to us that they will not vote for you. They are not breaking commitments to you; you have broken commitments to them.

You have too often casually prescribed nuclear war as a solution to a troubled world. You have too often stood for irresponsibility in the serious question of racial holocaust. You have too often read Taft and Eisenhower and Lincoln out of the Republican Party.

And that brings me to the second count of which the Republican Party is fighting for its soul. In the last few days the ill-advised efforts to make us stand for Goldwaterism instead of Republicanism has set off ripples of public opinion across the nation. All of us in San Francisco are so close to the hour-by-hour story unfolding here, that there is a danger we may overlook the overall impression being created in the minds of the American people. Goldwaterism has come to stand for keeping the views of Eisenhower out of our platform. Goldwaterism has come to stand for refusing to stand for law and order in maintaining racial peace. In short, Goldwaterism has come to stand for a whole crazy-quilt collection of absurd and dangerous positions that would be soundly repudiated by the American people in November.

Meanwhile, we have tried as best we can in the rigged situation engineered by your organization to articulate another point of view. These are not surface differences between you and the vast majority of Republicans. These are soul-deep differences over what the Republican Party stands for. We cannot lightly ignore the deep convictions of 60 per cent of the Republican Party that Goldwaterism is wrong. Circumstances have given me the responsibility of speaking up for their position. Inclination has given you the task of defending far different opinions. Neither of us can ignore our responsibilities.

I feel that I have nothing to fear from the Convention or from the millions of Americans watching it because my position is a right one. Certainly you should not fear a Convention you claim to control, and I would hope that we have not reached the point where you fear to face the nation. Therefore, I am asking that you join me in a request to allow both of us to appear before the Convention on Wednesday prior to the nominat-

52

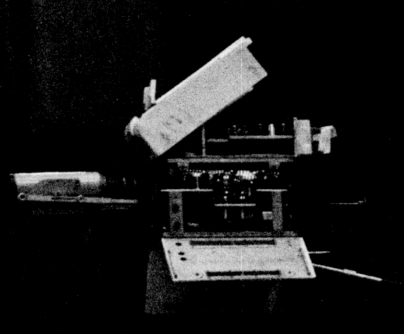

ing speeches. Each of us should be permitted to speak on the issues. Then we ought to have the opportunity to question each other. Frankly, few people expect that you will accept my invitation. If that is true, the implication will be quite clear: you have taken comfort in the inflated claims of your managers and you no longer have any regard for the opinions of uncommitted delegates or of the American public. So, it is up to you. You must decide whether the Goldwater philosophy can stand public examination—before the Convention and before the nation.

Sincerely yours, William W. Scranton.

---

*S*en. *Goldwater, angered by the letter, returns it to the Governor. The Senator's staff—believing the letter will backfire against Gov. Scranton—distributes a copy to every delegate in San Francisco.*

FIRST SESSION, JULY 13

BRINKLEY: As this first session opens here in the Cow Palace, located in Daly City just outside of San Francisco, many delegates are not in their seats. Probably some are still waiting for hotel elevators. This morning, as Sen. Goldwater was about to drive off from his headquarters at the Mark Hopkins Hotel, he was interviewed by NBC's Bob Teague.

TEAGUE: Senator, how does a candidate feel as the moment of decision approaches?

GOLDWATER: Scared to death. But very honored.

HUNTLEY: In the past 24 hours, the Scranton forces here have opened four new fronts.

One: the Governor has challenged Sen. Goldwater to a debate before this Convention. All Goldwater has to do to stop that is to say "No." Two: Scranton's forces plan to come to the floor with platform changes. Three: they will try to amend the Convention rules to bar delegates if there is evidence of racial discrimination in their selection. Four: they will demand a rules change to permit secret balloting for the nominees.

Sen. Goldwater appears to hope that he can coalesce the dissidents not only within the Republican Party, but within the Democratic Party as well. He has said, very candidly, that there are great Republican opportunities in the South. What we are talking about is a possible realignment of our two political parties, and it is going to bear watching.

Most significant developments occur not on the rostrum, but on the Convention floor and elsewhere throughout the city where political leaders formulate their strategy, hold their meetings and talk to reporters. Throughout the Convention, therefore, NBC newsmen concentrate on behind-the-scenes reports and floor interviews with political figures—in addition to covering the formal proceedings from the rostrum.

NEWMAN: I'm with former Sen. William Knowland, Chairman of the California delegation, and Goldwater's California campaign manager. Sir, what is your feeling about Gov. Scranton's letter?
KNOWLAND: It was an indication of desperation. There was never such an ill-tempered letter, in such poor taste, put out by a purported leader of either political Party against the leading contender of that Party. For Gov. Scranton to think that he has either the stature or the appeal to get delegates to violate their pledges is really questioning their integrity. He hasn't hurt Sen. Goldwater a bit; he's hurt himself. I say it more in sorrow than in anger, because I'm sorry to see a man like Gov. Scranton get sold a bill of goods by his Madison Avenue publicity advisers.

At 10:35 am, PDT, the first session is called to order by Rep. William Miller of New York, Chairman of the Republican National Committee. This is the first of two sessions today. The opening meeting is filled with formalities: official greetings by Mayor John F. Shelley of San Francisco; speeches by Sen. Thomas Kuchel of California, Gov. Tim Babcock of Montana and other Republican notables; a speech by the winner of the American Legion oratorical contest; the appointment of committees; and the election of the temporary chairman. As these opening ceremonies proceed on the rostrum, the political maneuvering continues elsewhere. Outside the Cow Palace,

pickets demonstrate against the nomination of Sen. Goldwater, and for a stronger civil rights plank. Inside, Gov. Romney of Michigan talks to Edwin Newman.

NEWMAN: What are your views of the platform?
ROMNEY: I think it's good but it has two deficiencies. We have ignored the real problem of extremism. And the civil rights position is incomplete.
NEWMAN: Can you be specific about extremism?
ROMNEY: The platform should indicate that every individual should have the right to dissent and to express his personal viewpoint. It should also state that we are opposed to individuals or groups of the Right or the Left who seek to infiltrate political parties or attach themselves to political candidates, like parasites, in order to accomplish the purpose of outside organizations rather than of the Party itself.

Scranton backers probe for weaknesses in the Goldwater front, hoping to stir a fight that could lead to delegate defections. A series of floor interviews reveals the widening split on the civil rights issue.

CHANCELLOR: The Scranton forces hope to gain votes by fighting over the seating of delegates. Here in the Tennessee delegation there's a battle over Lt. George W. Lee, a Memphis insurance broker who's a Negro. He has been to the four previous Republican Conventions, but was not chosen for this one by his delegation. The Chairman of the Tennessee delegation, George Ed Wilson, is here to explain his side of the story. [To Wilson]: The Scranton people say you kept Lt. Lee off because he was colored.
WILSON: That is absolutely untrue. This is a local contest in Shelby County and the City of Memphis. Lt. Lee's side and the other side were heard by the Executive Committee, which ruled almost unanimously in favor of the other delegates.

VANOCUR: I am with the Chairman of the Maryland delegation, Newton Steers, a Scranton supporter. What amendment are you going to introduce in this Convention?

STEERS: I advocate replacing any delegate who was elected by unfair procedures. The essence of this Convention is that it be fair—and it cannot be fair unless it, itself, is constituted in a fair manner.

VANOCUR: Are you talking specifically about Mr. Lee, the Negro delegate from Memphis?

STEERS: Lt. Lee would certainly appear to fall under this rule, and it will be up to the Credentials Committee to determine whether or not he does.

McGEE: Here is Sen. John Tower of Texas, a staunch supporter of Sen. Goldwater. What are you going to do about the proposed rule to bar any Republican delegation in whose selection discrimination has played a role?

TOWER: I don't think discrimination has been practiced in the selection of any delegation—and such a rule would leave the implication that discrimination had been practiced. Further, I believe it would open every delegation in the Convention to contest, and delay the Convention days and days. I think it's foolish and unnecessary.

VANOCUR: With me now is Mr. Chester Gillespie, a Negro with the Ohio delegation. Is it true that you walked out of the Ohio meeting this morning?

GILLESPIE: I did, because I think the nomination of Mr. Goldwater is tantamount to driving every Negro in the United States out of the Republican Party. This Party, in my opinion, is going to die, because there's no longer any reason for its existence. The cheers for Sen. Goldwater before the Platform Committee Friday night were not so much for him as they were anti-Negro. I don't think Negroes are welcome here. They're figuring on the white backlash, but I think Goldwater is going to be disappointed. The American people have more sense than to follow that kind of leadership. I have given of my time, of my heart, of my substance through 40 years, and I feel that I have been driven from the Party.

CHANCELLOR: Of the 2,316 delegates and alternates at this Convention, NBC has so far counted 25 Negro delegates and alternates. There was some feeling earlier that all the Negroes—at one dra-

matic moment during the Convention—might walk out. Two moments were considered dramatic enough for such a move: First, upon the approval of the present civil rights plank. Second, at the moment of Barry Goldwater's nomination. I have been polling many Negro delegates and alternates this morning, and it now seems likely that there won't be any kind of mass walkout.

Shortly after noon, the first test between the opposing forces occurs on the Convention floor. Newton Steers formally proposes his anti-discrimination rules change. On a voice vote, his proposal is shouted down by the delegates in a storm of noes.

HUNTLEY: The old rules prevail. The new rule was rejected. That is certainly another defeat for the Scranton forces. If this was a test, as it appears, then they got the answer. They were defeated.

Even as the Steers proposal is being voted down, Gov. Scranton addresses a crowd in San Francisco's Union Square. He is introduced by John Eisenhower, the former President's son, who is later interviewed by NBC on his role as a Scranton backer.

QUESTION: Mr. Eisenhower, did you decide to support Gov. Scranton on your own, or did you consult your father?

JOHN EISENHOWER: I did it completely on my own, in order to be direct and fair.

QUESTION: Why are you for Gov. Scranton?

JOHN EISENHOWER: He's a fine friend of mine, and I think he's been a magnificent Governor of Pennsylvania. He stands for exactly the same things that my father's administration stood for.

QUESTION: When it's all over, do you think you'll find unity among the Eisenhowers as the Republicans hope to find unity here?

JOHN EISENHOWER: We will find unity. Whoever is the nominee, we will all be behind him.

BRINKLEY: Gov. Scranton appears not to be terrified by Goldwater's delegate strength, which is now put at 800 by the Senator himself and 772 by NBC's delegate count. Scranton said, "We're in

an uphill fight, but we will never give up, because we are right." No one knows exactly how many will be nominated for President on Wednesday. There will be Goldwater, Scranton, Rockefeller, Sen. Fong of Hawaii and some Favorite Sons. Nominating speeches are supposed to be held to ten minutes, seconding speeches to three minutes. If they abide by that, it will be one of the great miracles of our lifetime.

HUNTLEY: At least three delegates from Gov. Scranton's own State of Pennsylvania are prepared to ask their chairman to release the delegation from its pledge to the Governor. They have candidly said that Scranton's cause is hopeless, and they don't want to be left out in the cold.

The first session ends with a reminder that the Convention will reconvene in the Cow Palace that same evening. As the delegates file out, NBC's floor correspondents summarize the situation.

VANOCUR: There is a great difference between the Goldwater and Scranton forces—and it isn't just that the Goldwater people have the votes. It's that the Goldwater people are as well organized as any group I've ever seen at a Convention. When Sen. Carl Curtis got up this morning and said he would vote "No" on the Steers amendment, that was the signal for the Goldwater delegates to vote "No" on the Steers amendment. These people have taken over John F. Kennedy's technique and perfected it. The Scranton forces, on the other hand, are not well organized at all. Their leaders have a great deal of difficulty making their positions known to their supporters.

CHANCELLOR: It was interesting to observe those who are reluctantly for Goldwater—men who must support him here and then go home to run on tickets with him. Some will tell you privately that they don't think they'll do very well if Sen. Goldwater is the nominee. Politics can trap you as well as anything else—and it has trapped them.

McGEE: There was, on the part of the Scranton people today, an air of rueful resignation. In the only scrap they had this morning, they knew be-

forehand that they were going to be defeated. And putting personal political connotation aside, it's sad to see any group of people trying to take consolation from how badly and quickly they are beaten, hoping that their utter defeat can in some way generate sympathy for their cause.

HUNTLEY: Now, for a summary of the coming contest over the platform, let's switch to Elie Abel.

ABEL: What could be the bitterest floor fight of this Convention is shaping up for tomorrow when the full platform comes before the delegates for their approval. The fight is bound to center first on civil rights, far and away the most emotional issue before this Convention and before this country. Scranton's floor manager, Sen. Scott of Pennsylvania, predicts a struggle for what he calls "the soul of the Republican Party." The Scranton people argue that the civil rights law will have to be enforced, and therefore the Republican candidate for President ought to be committed to enforcing it with all the powers at his command.

Although the floor fight plan of the Scranton forces has not been announced, there may also be demands for a specific denunciation of extremist groups such as the John Birch Society, and an explicit statement that the President and the President alone should decide when and whether this country would use nuclear weapons. The platform approved by the Resolutions Committee in the gray dawn of Sunday has nothing much to say on either of these points. To have written them into the platform as Gov. Scranton demanded would have amounted to censuring Sen. Goldwater, and the Goldwater people, of course, were in comfortable control of the platform writing committee. It didn't happen there, and the odds are against its happening on the Convention floor. The Senator from Arizona has refused time after time to condemn the John Birch Society. He also has advocated at various times, and in language that was less than consistent, more leeway for subordinate commanders in deciding to answer a Communist attack with nuclear weapons.

Although Gov. Scranton keeps saying the game is not over by any means, his backers privately

concede that it will take a miracle to bring off these platform changes. Whatever the outcome, they will have taken a stand for the future.

In mid-afternoon, former President Dwight Eisenhower holds a news conference that ranges over many subjects. He maintains his neutrality on the candidates, but heartens Goldwater's backers by saying that he does not feel the Senator's nomination would "represent a turning point in the history of the Republican Party." He also opposes an anti-extremist plank in the platform — a plank advocated by the Scranton forces. Primarily, he says he wants to play a unifying role for all shades of opinions within the Party. It is another setback for those Scranton supporters who had clung to the belief that Gen. Eisenhower would come out for their man.

SECOND SESSION, JULY 13

BRINKLEY: Tonight's principal business is the Keynote Address by Oregon's Gov. Mark Hatfield. It's supposed to whip up the Republicans — the kind of speech that in any other setting would end, "All right, men, now get out there and sell."

HUNTLEY: The Rules Committee has just voted down a pro-Scranton motion to require secret ballots when the delegations are polled for the Presidential nominee. Another defeat for the Scranton forces. Meanwhile, Gov. Scranton's now celebrated letter is rapidly becoming a classic of this Convention — and indeed is on its way to becoming the most provocative development of the entire week. Now, NBC's Tom Pettit talks to the Governor about that letter:

PETTIT: Do you stand on the letter as written?

SCRANTON: Yes, this is entirely my responsibility, and I stand on it...I did not write the letter, and I did not read it before it was sent. Also, I did not sign it. But, in the course of that Sunday — when I was running around speaking to a lot of delegations — I did authorize the sending of a letter on the basis that I wished to challenge Sen. Goldwater to be with me before the Convention to outline our thinking on three major issues. One is the use of nuclear weapons and who should have authority over same. Sen. Goldwater has indicated that he would be more willing to use these than most people think is reasonable. Second, the matter of extremism and the efforts on the extremists' part to take over our Party. I think that is much more important in the long run than the nominees. And third, the matter of the civil rights law and the possible extension of difficulties in its enforcement or lack of enforcement.

PETTIT: Do you think the letter, as written by your staff, was too strongly worded?

SCRANTON: I think it is probably too strongly worded. I'll be honest with you. I think it's stronger than the kind of language I would use. I think this is why the rumors got around that I had not written it. People who know me well know I don't use this kind of language. But I must say to you that I feel very strongly that these most unfortunate opinions and attitudes on the part of Sen. Goldwater should be brought to the attention of the public.

PETTIT: Does this amount to a kind of apology for the strongness of the language?

SCRANTON: No, I don't apologize for anything that has been done that's my responsibility.

BRINKLEY: I don't remember anything comparable to this even in the Taft-Eisenhower Convention in 1952. The Taft-Eisenhower fight got pretty messy for awhile, though I don't remember anybody calling anyone else names quite as ugly as those used by Gov. Scranton.

MacNEIL [from the Mark Hopkins Hotel]: As it's turning out, Scranton's letter has been the one thing he could have done to make Goldwater's nomination certain — short of withdrawing altogether. There's been a conspicuous movement of delegates to Goldwater today, at least some of it attributable either to anger at the letter or to an intimation that the letter was a move of desperation and therefore smelled of defeatism. The Goldwater people have been puzzling over the Governor's motives in sending the letter. One new hypothesis is that the letter is really aimed at next

November. The reasoning is that Scranton expects Goldwater to be nominated, but soundly defeated by Lyndon Johnson. Thus, the letter, with its extremely sharp choice of words, is designed to open an unbridgeable chasm between the two. That would leave the Republican liberals free to tell Goldwater we-told-you-so, and attempt to take the Party's leadership back after November.

HUNTLEY: A comparison of the 1960 and 1964 Republican platforms graphically demonstrates the change that has occurred in Party philosophy in the past four years.

In 1960, the platform endorsed general Federal aid for school construction. This year it calls for limited, selective aid for higher education.

The 1960 platform noted with pride the Eisenhower administration's progress in protecting consumers against harmful food, drugs and cosmetics. This year the platform pledges an end to what it calls the ceaseless pressing by the White House, the Food and Drug Administration and Federal Trade Commission, to dominate consumer decisions in the marketplace. That is a turn of almost 180 degrees.

On immigration, the 1960 plank advocated doubling the number of immigrants admitted each year, and the use of the 1960 census instead of the 1920 census as a legal basis. This platform supports only legislation seeking to reunite families.

The 1960 civil rights plank was notably broad, and pledged action against discrimination in Federally aided housing. It said, "We reaffirm the constitutional right to peaceable assembly, to protest discrimination by private business establishments." This was beaten this year. The only 1964 sentence seemingly referring to civil rights demonstrations accuses the Administration of encouraging disorderly and lawless elements.

In foreign policy, the two platforms differ sharply. The 1960 plank praised cultural exchanges and the United States-Soviet agreement for neutral Antarctica. It expressed deep concern about the mounting nuclear arms race and expressed readiness to negotiate for disarmament.

67

In 1964, it emphasizes caution in disarmament and in negotiations with Communists.

Where the 1960 plank spoke of a just settlement for the reduction of world tensions, the 1964 platform says that in negotiating we will never abandon insistence on advantages for the free world. Instead of defense against Communist aggression, it speaks of victory over Communism.

BRINKLEY: On the Convention floor, the keynote speaker has just been introduced—Gov. Mark Hatfield of Oregon, perhaps the handsomest man in either political Party.

HIGHLIGHTS FROM GOV. HATFIELD'S ADDRESS

The Republican Party is committed to a set of principles. This commitment is an act of unwavering faith in the American people, in the cause of freedom, in the eternal principles of morality, and there is a stark contrast in the record of the present administration.

In place of faith, we find fear. Anxieties and tensions infect and corrupt our country. At least three fears have typified this administration: fear of the facts, fear of the future and fear of the people. We ask you, was it a Republican administration that presided over the fiasco of the Bay of Pigs? Was it a Republican administration that neutralized Laos and so initiated a chain of events that threatens freedom throughout all of Southeast Asia? And I ask you, was it a Republican administration that ignored the problem in Cuba until it erupted into rioting and bloodshed? Was it a Republican administration in power when the Berlin wall was built?

You know, and all Americans know, that these things have happened under the misrule of the opposition in the past four years.

The Republican Party offers Americans a choice—a choice between fear and faith. We have faith in the forces of law and order under our Constitution. Our faith challenges any who would destroy freedom whether they wrap themselves in a false cloak of patriotism or an equally false

69

cloak of religion. There are bigots in this nation who spew forth their venom of hate. They parade under hundreds of labels, including the Communist Party, the Ku Klux Klan and the John Birch Society. They must be overcome...

HUNTLEY: Gov. Hatfield's reference to the Ku Klux Klan, the Communist Party and the John Birch Society was not received graciously or enthusiastically on the floor of the Convention. As a matter of fact, there was some booing at that point.

BRINKLEY: Gov. Hatfield was not the choice of the Goldwater people for keynoter. They wanted William Miller, the National Chairman. But Miller said he didn't want to do it, that he had too much to do. While the Goldwater people were trying to think of somebody else, Hatfield was slipped in.

ABERNETHY: With me is Dr. Milton Eisenhower.

MILTON EISENHOWER: I was exceedingly impressed with all of Gov. Hatfield's address this evening, and I was particularly happy when he condemned extremism in all its forms. We Americans have a tendency to condemn the extremism of the Left, then we forget that that of the Right is very similar in character and equally dangerous to our society. He brought it out in the open, and I was delighted when he got an ovation from the audience when he made his point.

ABERNETHY: Do you see this Convention as one in which extremism is a real issue?

MILTON EISENHOWER: It's a part of the issue. As a matter of fact, I think there is a big misunderstanding in this Convention. It's assumed that the supporters of one nominee are conservatives, and the supporters of another nominee are liberals. I don't think this is a test between conservatives and liberals. I think most Republicans are genuine conservatives. Perhaps the better description is between a negative attitude and a positive attitude toward the very complex domestic and international problems of our time.

HUNTLEY: The session has concluded. We have

had a rather full day. The Convention was called to order about 35 minutes after its appointed time, and we soon had the first big fight. It was over Newton Steers' anti-discriminatory proposal—and the Scranton forces were slapped down. Another fight is coming up tomorrow when the Scranton forces bring in their amendment to the platform.

THIRD SESSION, JULY 14

At 10:35 am, PDT, former Vice President Richard Nixon arrives in San Francisco. At a news conference, he contends that the platform, as written, "is big enough for all Republicans to support, and big enough for Goldwater to campaign on." Mr. Nixon, assuming the role of peacemaker, repeatedly defends Sen. Goldwater, praising "his very refreshing candor," and asserting that the Senator "has been a reasonable man, he has been a moderate man, and he has insisted on his principles." At 4:30 pm, PDT, Gov. Mark Hatfield calls the Republican Convention's third session to order.

HUNTLEY: Today's session should be extremely important. On the agenda are an address by former President Dwight Eisenhower, and the report of the Platform Committee. The report will touch off some action on the floor, because the Scranton moderate forces are coming in with three additions which they will propose for the platform. One: they want it clearly stated that only the President of the United States shall have ultimate command over all nuclear weapons. Two: they want a stronger commitment to the Civil Rights Act. Three: they wish to condemn extremist groups, such as the John Birch Society.

McGEE: Talking about the platform, where Scranton has chosen to make his final stand, Goldwater said, "What the minority cannot get through their heads is that this is a true representation of the thinking of the Republican Party."

The increasingly bitter struggle between the Scranton and Goldwater forces is brought into dramatic focus by contrasting interviews with two leading spokesmen: Ambassador Henry Cabot Lodge for the

Scranton forces and Sen. John Tower of Texas for the Goldwater majority.

HARKNESS: How can you stay within the Republican Party with such a platform?

LODGE: Oh, well, you can't agree with everything that your Party does. I have been a Republican all my life, and I'm not going to let this crowd, many of whom have only been Republican for three years, throw me out. I intend to stay in the Party and continue to work for the kind of Republican Party that I believe in.

NEWMAN [to Sen. Tower]: The Scranton forces plan to make a floor fight tonight on the issue of extremism. They want to name the Communists, the Ku Klux Klan and the John Birch Society as organizations that the Republican Party deplores. What would be the objection to doing that?

TOWER: If you're going to start naming organizations, there are a number of others that are far more dangerous than the John Birch Society — those that are subversive in character, those that are front organizations—you'd have a very lengthy platform if you tried to name all of them. This is nothing the government can solve. It has to be resolved in the hearts of men.

NEWMAN: The suggestion is often made that there are extremist forces attached to Sen. Goldwater.

TOWER: This is completely untrue. Sen. Goldwater has been meticulous in his efforts to make sure that all of his managers and leaders were responsible Republicans.

At 5:36 pm, PDT, Sen. Thruston Morton of Kentucky becomes the Convention's Permanent Chairman. He vigorously attacks the Democratic administration, aiming especially at the Bobby Baker and the Billie Sol Estes cases. Then, Charles Halleck of Indiana, Minority Leader of the House of Representatives, introduces former President Eisenhower, who receives a rousing ovation. President Eisenhower pleads for unity, warning Republicans not to "drown in a whirlpool of factional strife and divisive ambitions." He calls on the Party to "scorn the divisive efforts of those outside our family—including sensation-seeking columnists and commentators—because,

my friends, I assure you that these are people who couldn't care less about the good of our Party."

This brings the delegates leaping to their feet with an explosion of cheers and applause for President Eisenhower and boos and catcalls for the reporters on the Convention floor. Many shake their fists at the newsmen in the glassed-in television and radio booths.

President Eisenhower also counsels his Party to reject "as unfit and unwholesome all who are purveyors of hatred and intolerance, who are prone to the use of violence, who malign the character of fellow Americans and who baselessly charge decent Americans with treasonable acts or intentions." The former President is again cheered when he says: "Let us not be guilty of maudlin sympathy for the criminal who, roaming the streets with switchblade knife and illegal firearms seeking a helpless prey, suddenly becomes—upon apprehension—a poor, underprivileged person who counts upon the compassion of our society and the laxness or weakness of too many courts to forgive his offense." Speaking of the Civil Rights Act, President Eisenhower tells the country: "I want to give you something very definitely from my heart. With the passage of this law, I believe that every Republican should now take upon himself a moral commitment to do his utmost to see that this law is implemented not merely by power of legally constituted enforcement agencies, but by the hearts of a determined and free people."

At 7:00 pm, PDT, Rep. Laird, Chairman of the Platform Committee, announces that the entire Republican platform will be read aloud. The Scranton people believe this maneuver is designed to delay the floor fight until television viewers in the East have retired. Almost two hours are consumed in reading the 8,500-word document, and it will be almost midnight in the East before the reading ends.

HUNTLEY: There is no one unhappier here than the Eastern progressive Republicans. They see their Party inheriting the unmeasured opposition to the new gains of the Negro in civil rights. They acknowledge that this issue is going to skirt the fragile boundaries of racism—and that the campaign could spill over into that dark and foreboding area. Eastern leaders also acknowledge that their Party in 1964 will reflect the nostalgic yearning for a return to the simplicity of a frontier society, where there were no Social Security numbers, no labor contracts, no welfare bureaus, and where government—like the discouraging word—was seldom heard. Eastern Republicans are per-

turbed by the new Republican money which has carried the Goldwater campaign to this crowning success. It's Texas money, Southern California, Arizona, Utah, Colorado and some Southern money. It has no patina of quiet reserve and great dignity. It is new and shiny money, and it rings with brashness on the political counter. The Eastern Republicans—who have associates, friends or investments in Europe—are accustomed to looking across the Atlantic. They are uneasy about this new Republicanism of the West, which frequently feels that the primary interest of the United States lies not in Europe, but in the Far East. The Eastern, progressive, industrialized Republican is not a happy Republican here tonight. His Party has been picked up and carried across the Southern and Western horizons.

BRINKLEY: That's especially interesting in view of the fact that they didn't find it out until very lately. At the GOP Convention in 1960, after Nixon was nominated, Goldwater himself took the rostrum and said, "Let's grow up, conservatives. We want to take this Party back, and someday I think we can." He then proceeded to urge the conservative Republicans to get behind him as their leader, and they did, with the result we are seeing here now. He started his campaign four years ago, but for some reason Republicans opposed to Goldwater took an awful long time to discover it. At one point, Sen. Javits—who is an Eastern Republican opposed to Goldwater—said Goldwater's conservatism satisfies a national hankering for a nickel beer and a nickel cigar. He said this is nice and old-fashioned, but it doesn't belong today.

Well, whether it belongs today or not, if that is what the Goldwater people seek, it's been attractive enough for them to have worked fervently for four years, and to have brought their man here with an almost unbeatable lead.

A t 8:30 pm, PDT, while the platform reading continues, an incident occurs that resembles a scene from a comic opera, but it has significant overtones. It begins when David Brinkley asks NBC's John Chancellor to "come in" with his interview from the Alaska delegation.

CHANCELLOR: I'd come in if I could, David, but I may be under arrest. They have been trying to clear the aisles here—an understandable problem at a place like the Cow Palace, with all the people on the floor. We were waiting to do an interview in the Alaska delegation when two sergeants at arms came along and said, "You'll have to clear the aisle." We said we were working, and they said that didn't make any difference to them, so I sat down. Whereupon a policeman, Badge No. 21, from the Daly City police, tried to eject me forcibly. Am I going to be carried out?

ANSWER: You'll be removed by orders of the sergeant at arms.

CHANCELLOR: I wonder if I could get your name?

ANSWER: My name is Gary Kidwell.

CHANCELLOR: Okay. I don't want to debate this with you, Mr. Kidwell — let's get on with it. I'm about to be removed. Go ahead, gentlemen, remove. I'd just like to have one reason. Mr. Kidwell doesn't have a very nice job trying to get the reporters out. I can never remember a Convention staff being asked to clear the aisles of the press.

VANOCUR: I don't mean to interrupt, John. I'm standing by Puerto Rico, where there was a little fracas. The sergeants at arms are under instructions to get us out of here. This has been going on now for three days, and tonight I think it reached a climax. A photographer from LIFE tried to get in, and they just pushed him back. Now we're having a little altercation here between a sergeant at arms and an NBC light man and things are a bit sticky back here at the moment.

CHAIRMAN MORTON: Break up this demonstration or whatever is going on over here! Sergeant at arms, clear the aisles over there!

VANOCUR: My instructions from my NBC desk are to withdraw in good order, and in good order I will now withdraw.

CHANCELLOR: There's another policeman here, Badge No. 38; he's got a hand on my elbow, and there's a sheriff's policeman coming forward. Here we go, down the middle aisle. It's hard to be dignified at a time like this. Well, I don't know what to say. What do you say? I'm in custody. I've been promised bail, ladies and gentlemen, by my office. This way, officer? Up this way. And for those of you who are watching, I want to assure you that NBC is fully staffed with other reporters who are not in the custody of the Daly City police and the San Mateo sheriff's office. I formally say that this is a disgrace. The press, radio and television should be allowed to do their work at a Convention. I'm being taken down off the arena now, by these policemen, and I'll check in later. This is John Chancellor, somewhere in custody.

BRINKLEY [laughing]: John, call us when you can, and let us hear from you, often. That's the silliest thing I've ever seen in my life, and I've seen a lot of silly things. The aisles are clogged from one end of the hall to the other with every kind of obstruction—and the only one they can find to arrest is John Chancellor, who is really a mild and inoffensive fellow.

HUNTLEY: I think this was a first, a man broadcasting his own arrest on television.

BRINKLEY: And I hope a last.

HUNTLEY: All this stems from the attitude of this Convention toward the press. This ugliness has persisted all week, and it's just beginning to flare up on the floor. Meanwhile, the reading of the platform goes on.

BRINKLEY: What were they reading in the platform while that was happening?

HUNTLEY: How to preserve the peace, I think.

BRINKLEY: I don't know what they would charge John with. It couldn't be vagrancy, because I know he's got money in his pocket.

BRINKLEY [a short time later]: The chief sergeant at arms of the Republican Convention is now escorting John Chancellor back to the floor, and I can hardly wait to see him. It really was pretty silly. If they wanted to clear the aisles, nobody would object, but they haven't. I never have and, I assume, never will see a clear aisle at a Convention. I think they are worse than they were before the instructions were given out.

HUNTLEY: We understand that John Chancellor is ready to broadcast, and he's going to interview the sergeant at arms. Come in, John.

CHANCELLOR: As I was saying—we were escorted off the floor by the policeman from the San Mateo County sheriff's office and the Daly City police, whereupon we met Mr. Robert Carter, who's the chief sergeant at arms of this Convention, and a gentleman we've known before. And, Bob, you said that you would escort me back on the floor and there were no hard feelings.

CARTER: None whatsoever. We were trying to clear the aisles so we could continue an orderly Convention. After we have them cleared, we'll let the people who have legitimate access to the aisles back on them, and we're sure that John Chancellor will be one of the first back.

With the reading of the platform completed at 8:50 pm, PDT (11:50 pm in the East), Rep. Laird asks the Convention to approve it as written. But the Scranton forces are determined to present their alternatives, and the long awaited floor fight is on.

Sen. Hugh Scott of Pennsylvania, one of Gov. Scranton's top lieutenants, presents the proposal to condemn extremist groups by name: the John Birch Society, the Communists and the Ku Klux Klan. First to speak in support of the amendment is Gov. Rockefeller, who is greeted by a chorus of boos from many of the delegates on the floor, and by what appears to be virtually everyone in the galleries. The Governor cannot make himself heard over the catcalls. Chairman Morton repeatedly gavels for quiet, but without success. Finally, his patience worn by the outburst, the Governor calls out: "Some of you don't like to hear it, ladies and gentlemen, but it's the truth." He urges the delegates to repudiate the extremes of the political Left and Right, but his voice is drowned out. Two speakers follow Rockefeller, urging adoption of the amendment to condemn extremist groups, and three advocate its defeat. On a voice vote, it is thunderously defeated.

Gov. Romney then proposes a milder amendment on extremism—this one avoiding citing any group by name—but his plea, passionately delivered, is also defeated.

At 9:54 pm, PDT (12:54 am in the East), Sen. Scott offers an amendment strengthening the civil rights plank. Ten speakers—five for and five against—mount the rostrum. Among those speaking against the proposal is Rep. William McCulloch of Ohio, who was one of the leaders for the Civil Rights Act passed by the Congress. Sen. Scott's amendment is beaten on a roll call, 879 to 409. For the first time, the actual strength of the Goldwater camp is revealed.

It is 11:20 pm, PDT (2:20 am in the East), when the prin-

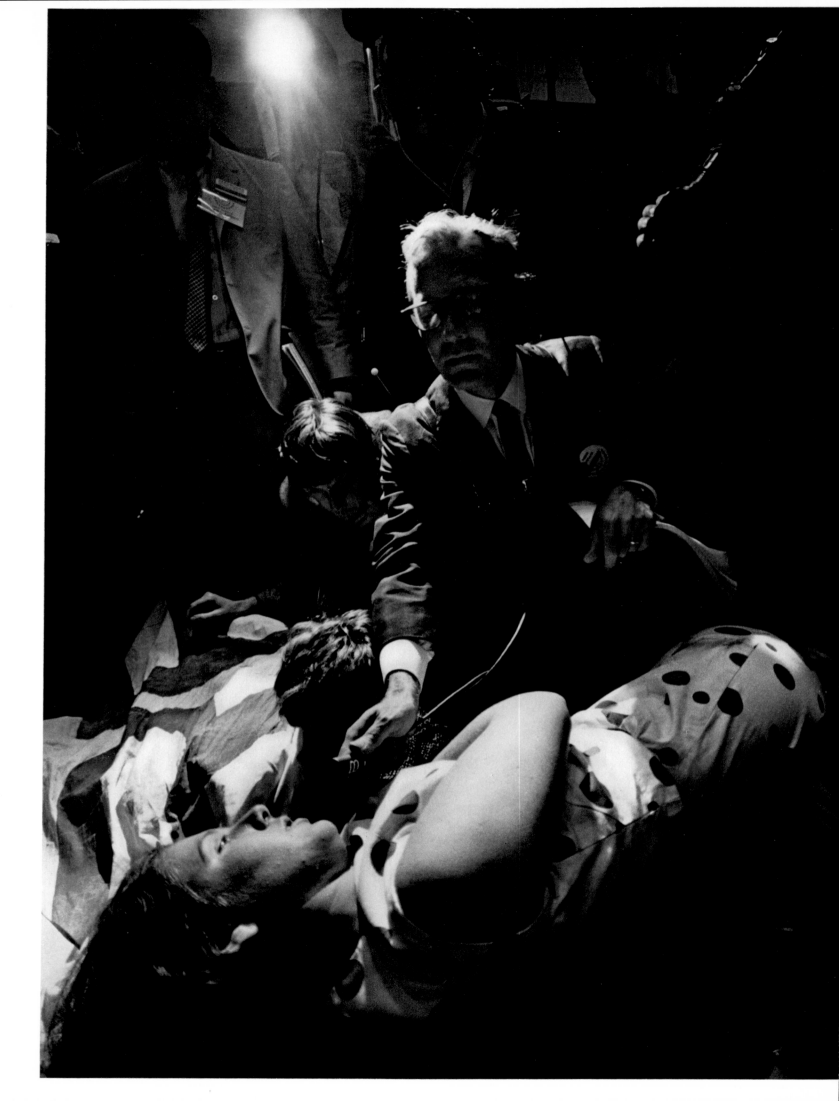

cipal advocate of Gov. Scranton's third proposal addresses the Convention. He is Christian Herter, Secretary of State under President Eisenhower, who urges the delegates to add to the platform the principle that only the President shall have the power to decide when and how nuclear weapons are to be used. At 12:17 am, the amendment is defeated by a voice vote.

At 12:34 am, PDT (3:34 am in the East), the Republican Platform is adopted as originally written — and four minutes later the session is adjourned. The delegates have been in the hall for more than eight hours.

Outside, civil rights pickets chant, sing, and attempt to block the exits and to snarl traffic. But the delegates are able to leave with a minimum of interference.

FOURTH SESSION, JULY 15

HUNTLEY: This is the fourth, and in many ways the culminating session of the Republican Convention. Before this day is out, the nominee of the Republican Party will have been determined.

BRINKLEY: Today there will be a speech by George Murphy, the former movie star who is running for the Senate against Pierre Salinger in California; then the roll-call of the States for nominations and nominating speeches; then the demonstrations, which will be spectacular; and finally, the voting for a nominee. They will try to move along rapidly so it will be done before everybody in the Eastern time zone goes to bed. Last night it ran so late the audience must have consisted entirely of insomniacs and night watchmen.

McGEE: The warring moderate and Right wings of the Republican Party are determined to battle it out to the bitter end — and all evidence to date suggests that it will be a bitter end.

Only former President Eisenhower is suggesting that Goldwater and Scranton would make a good ticket. Goldwater has said that he couldn't be comfortable with Scranton. During an impromptu news conference, Sen. Goldwater, who obviously has no further need to court the delegates, launched his campaign for the Presidency with a slashing attack on President Johnson.

QUESTION: Are you concerned about the Demo-crats taking advantage of the Republicans not approving a stronger civil rights plank?

GOLDWATER: Look. After Lyndon Johnson, the biggest faker in the United States, having opposed the Civil Rights Act for all the years of his life until this year, I'm not worried. Let them make an issue of it. I'll just recite the thousands of words he's spoken for the poll tax, against FEPC, against equal accommodations, and against civil rights. This is the phoniest individual that ever came around.

McGEE: The talk of a Vice Presidential candidate is increasing, with the name of National Chairman William Miller popping up more than any of the others. Miller is not discouraging the talk, as witness this interview with NBC's Floyd Kalber.

KALBER: Mr. Miller, any contact at all from the Goldwater people?

MILLER: If you're referring to the Vice Presidency, nothing in connection with that. We've had many discussions with staff people, but I haven't talked to the Senator at all.

KALBER: You would accept it if he asked you, wouldn't you?

MILLER: Yes, I have said repeatedly that I'm a Republican who believes in my Party, and believes that it's the best instrument for good government. I'd do anything, and if the nominee should select me as his running mate, I would be honored, I would be delighted, and I would accept.

KALBER: How about describing your philosophy?

MILLER: I think you have to talk in terms of specifics when you get into philosophies. I found myself, in 14 years in the Congress, in odd company on odd days on odd issues for odd reasons. I have been labeled recently as a conservative, and yet, while I'm not wedded to these terms, I was also rated as being a very staunch supporter of the Eisenhower program.

KALBER: Would you say that your views are in accord with the Senator's?

MILLER: There are vast areas of agreement between me and the Senator. I am sure that he doesn't agree with me on everything, and I don't

agree with him on everything—but then, I don't agree with my wife on everything.

At 3:23 pm, PDT, Sen. Everett McKinley Dirksen of Illinois rises to nominate Sen. Goldwater. In mellifluous tones (reminiscent of an organ augmented by cellos, in David Brinkley's phrase), Sen. Dirksen hails "Barry Goldwater, the grandson of an immigrant frontier peddler," for his "quality of moral courage which has won him the admiration of the citizens of this land."

"Delegates to this Convention," Sen. Dirksen intones, "the tide is turning! Let's give one hundred and ninety million Americans the choice they have been waiting for!"

As the nominating speech comes to its end, the Cow Palace bursts into a frenzied demonstration. Banners, bands, gold balloons, paraders, pretty girls, delirious delegates, and noise devices of every description combine in a bedlam that goes on for 29 minutes.

NEWMAN: I am in front of the box occupied by Mrs. Barry Goldwater and her two daughters. Mrs. Goldwater, can you tell us how you feel?

MRS. GOLDWATER: Wonderful. It's so thrilling. So exciting. I can't hear you.

NEWMAN: Mrs. Goldwater, I think you said you can't hear me. I think the audience would like to know just what your feelings are at this moment.

MRS. GOLDWATER: Well, it's hard to tell you what my feelings are, but you must know that I'm very, very excited.

NEWMAN: Have you been waiting for this moment for a long, long time?

MRS. GOLDWATER: Yes, I have. Yes. A long time.

NEWMAN: Mrs. Goldwater, is this the proudest moment of your life?

MRS. GOLDWATER: Yes, I think it is.

NEWMAN: Thank you very much, Mrs. Goldwater.

BRINKLEY: I have just been informed that this portion of the Convention proceedings is being fed to Europe by satellite, and I have been asked to explain what is going on. I am afraid that is beyond my powers. It would be hard to explain it even to an American. As best as I can put it for Europeans, the Goldwater people, like those who will demonstrate later for other candidates, have been waiting for weeks and months and years to display in some outward, tangible way, how they feel about their candidate. When, finally, he was formally put in nomination, all of the pent-up energy, exuberance, noise, signs, slogans, bands and balloons suddenly were released. It is partly political, partly emotional, partly propaganda, partly a social mechanism, partly a carnival, and partly mass hysteria. It can be described as nonsense, and often is—but somehow it works.

As the bedlam continues, Chairman Morton goodnaturedly tells the demonstrators to come to order or their man will never get nominated. With order finally restored, Sen. Goldwater's nomination is seconded by former Sen. William Knowland, Mrs. Clare Boothe Luce, Sen. John Tower, and Rep. Charles Halleck.

Seven others are nominated during the next five hours: Gov. Nelson Rockefeller of New York; Sen. Hiram Fong of Hawaii; Sen. Margaret Chase Smith of Maine; Gov. William Scranton of Pennsylvania; Gov. George Romney of Michigan; former Rep. Walter Judd of Minnesota; and Ambassador Henry Cabot Lodge of Massachusetts. Two of these are historic: Sen. Smith is the first woman ever nominated for President by either major Party, and Sen. Fong is the first person of Asian ancestry ever nominated.

Ambassador Lodge, who left San Francisco on Tuesday, sends a message from Boston asking that his name be withdrawn, and his request is honored. As the nominations continue, Mrs. Scranton talks to NBC's Richard Hunt.

MRS. SCRANTON: From what I've seen on television of what's happened at the Convention, I am convinced the doors have been manned by, and the galleries packed by the Goldwaterites. I am sorry the people of America do not have a choice.

HUNT: This has been a hard, fast, furious four weeks. If defeat comes, how are you going to feel?

MRS. SCRANTON: To the best of my belief I will feel as I do now: complete pride in Bill Scranton.

HUNT: Mrs. Scranton, is there any chance that your husband might take second place on the ticket?

MRS. SCRANTON: None.

HUNT: Even if Sen. Goldwater and President Eisenhower came to him and asked him to do it?

MRS. SCRANTON: The answer is NO, in capital letters. May I explain why? It is because Bill Scranton feels very strongly that a Party will not have

unity if one man is speaking in one way and another man is speaking in another way. There can't be two leaders of the Party. I know that no matter what happens, Bill Scranton will always stand tall and walk proudly.

At 10:14 pm, PDT, the roll call for the Republican Presidential nomination begins. Alabama leads off by giving its 20 votes to Sen. Goldwater—and he is never headed. When the roll call gets to South Carolina, the electronic scoreboard shows that this State could put him over the top. An enormous roar fills the hall. "Mr. Chairman! Mr. Chairman!" cries the South Carolina voice above the din. "Mr. Chairman, we are humble and grateful that we can do this for America. South Carolina casts 16 votes for Sen. Goldwater." Those votes give Sen. Goldwater 663—eight more than he needs for the nomination. The balloting concludes, with the final tally showing: Goldwater 883, Scranton 214, Rockefeller 114, Romney 41, Mrs. Smith 27, Judd 22, Fong 5, Lodge 2.

Gov. Scranton, who has been inside his VIP trailer since 9:00 pm, enters the hall and, elegant to the last, makes his way to the rostrum. The moment is too much for his 18-year-old daughter Susan, who joins in the applause for her father with tears running down her cheeks. From the rostrum, the Governor asks that the vote for Sen. Goldwater be made unanimous. Mindful of Sen. Goldwater's speech of capitulation and unification at the 1960 Convention—Gov. Scranton delivers an address of his own.

HIGHLIGHTS OF GOV. SCRANTON'S ADDRESS

Four years ago, another Republican stood where I stand now, and I think I know what was in his heart. He must have felt—as I do now—a renewed and humble gratitude for the ingenious way in which our free institutions allow a man, if he has but the courage, to stand in open and spirited defense of his own principles. But the time has come when an honorable man can say that the sense of this great Convention has become abundantly clear. Without compromising principle in the slightest, we can say that in this Convention our point of view has not prevailed. And so be the will of the Convention.

To those who have been so steadfast in their loyalty to me and to the principles for which we fought in common, I now say that the time has come for us to shift the scene of the battle. To the victor I extend my very warm congratulations. He has waged a long, hard campaign, and every man can applaud the labor that brought about the victory that is now his, just as I do now. The Republican Party—as it is here in Convention assembled and as it is across the length of this broad land—must now emphasize its unity, not its differences. We must now be about the business of defeating Democrats.

And I make this pledge to you. I shall put whatever campaigning talent I may have to the job of winning Republican victories on every level this fall. Some of us did not prevail at this Convention, but let it be clearly understood that this great Republican Party is our historic house. This is our home. Let us pledge not to desert our Party, but to strengthen it. I say: come, let us work within the Republican Party, not from outside it.

Now, beginning right from this moment, all of us Republicans must get on with the business of victory. Mr. Chairman, I have the privilege to move that we make the nomination of Sen. Goldwater unanimous.

HUNTLEY: The Republican Party is under new management. It is headed in a new direction, and precisely what that direction is will be more clearly defined during the course of the campaign. A case might be made in behalf of the proposition that this has been one of the most significant and meaningful Conventions of our time. One of our political Parties has been picked up, it has been given new management, and it has been set on an entirely new course — and that is an interesting thing to watch. And we will watch its last session right here tomorrow.

FIFTH SESSION, JULY 16

HUNTLEY: Today we'll hear a speech from Richard Nixon—whose function here in San Francisco is to bring all the warring factions together and send them into the campaign united and solidified.

Then there will be a speech by William Miller for the Vice Presidency, by Sen. Goldwater for the Presidency, and the formation of new committees as the Party organizes for another four years.

BRINKLEY: At his news conference today Gov. Scranton said among other things, "If I had it to do all over again, the only thing I would have done differently was to read the letter before it was sent." That letter did him serious harm. There's a button in circulation saying, "I would rather write than be President."

McGEE: Sen. Barry Goldwater, the Generalissimo of the Republican Party, assembled the old generals today and told them who the new generals will be. Party chairmen answered muster at Goldwater's headquarters, where he told them he had selected Congressman William Miller as his Vice Presidential running mate, and Dean Burch as National Chairman of the Republican Party, the post that Miller has held. Both are staunch conservatives—so after nearly a quarter of a century in the political wilderness, conservatives are again firmly in control of the Republican Party. The moderates—bruised, battered and beaten—are withdrawing from the field. Goldwater's running mate and the new Party Chairman are almost total strangers to the American public. Dean Burch is 36, a lawyer from Tucson, Arizona, and assistant general director of the Goldwater campaign for the nomination. He was once Goldwater's administrative assistant in Washington, and helped in the Senator's drive for the nomination against Nixon four years ago.

The Vice Presidential choice, William Miller, said in jest yesterday, "Barry is a Protestant and Jew, and I'm a Catholic. Anyone who's against that ticket is a damned bigot."

The session formally opens at 4:20 pm, PDT. Ten minutes later, Sen. Gordon Allott of Colorado nominates Rep. Miller for Vice President. No other candidate is presented. On a roll call vote, during which three Tennessee delegates pass, Miller is declared the unanimous choice, and he makes a brief acceptance speech.

89

I love this country with all my heart. I love this Party, the finest instrument for good government this country has ever known. I love the people of the United States of America. Two-hundred million strong, devoted to God, consecrated to liberty, and all crusaders for justice—all crusaders for equality of opportunity for every person on the face of the earth.

My family and I here pledge ourselves to you that we shall devote our hearts and our hands, our energies and our abilities, and our spirit and our enthusiasm, in this greatest challenge of my lifetime. And we shall do so every minute of every hour of every day from this point forward.

In this great common purpose, I now stand at the side of a man who, more than any other I have ever known in American life, speaks the truth to the people, courageously stands for principle and devotes himself completely to keeping America free—the great son of Arizona, Barry Goldwater.

ABEL: In the dying hours of this Republican Convention, we have seen once again that it is the Presidential candidate who chooses his running mate, apparently without regard to popular appeal or demonstrated capacity in national and international affairs. On the surface it would seem Sen. Goldwater chose Congressman Miller of upstate New York for geographical balance. Miller, as National Chairman of the Party, is well known among professional politicians across the country. He is a slashing campaigner, the partisan personified. He is, moreover, a Catholic. But Miller at this stage is far from being a national figure. Already, Congressmen and Senators from the Northeastern States, who are up for re-election in November, are saying that Miller's nomination will not help them overcome what they describe as the definite handicap of campaigning on the Goldwater ticket.

R*ep. Miller is followed to the rostrum by former Vice President Nixon, who makes a determined appeal for Party unity. He scorns the public opinion polls, which show President Johnson far ahead of Sen. Gold-*

water. "The only poll that counts is the one all of us will be voting in," he says, "and Mr. Gallup isn't going to be counting the votes, either." Mr. Nixon's address serves as the introduction to Sen. Goldwater, and when the Senator arrives in the Cow Palace, and makes his way to the rostrum accompanied by his wife, the hall resounds with a tremendous ovation—drums beat, balloons pour down from the ceiling, and "The Battle Hymn of the Republic" is played. For eight minutes the demonstration continues, and then the Senator delivers his acceptance address.

HIGHLIGHTS OF SEN. GOLDWATER'S ACCEPTANCE SPEECH

The Good Lord raised this mighty Republican Republic to be a home for the brave and to flourish as the land of the free—not to stagnate in the swampland of collectivism, not to cringe before the bully of communism.

The tide has been running against freedom. Our people have followed false prophets. We must, and we shall, return to proven ways—not because they are old, but because they are true.

During four futile years the administration which we shall replace has distorted and lost that faith. It has talked and talked and talked the words of freedom, but it has failed and failed and failed in the works of freedom.

Because of this administration we are tonight a world divided. We are a nation becalmed. We have lost the brisk pace of diversity and the genius of individual creativity. We are plodding along at a pace set by centralized planning, red tape, rules without responsibility, and regimentation without recourse.

Tonight there is violence in our streets, corruption in our highest offices, aimlessness among our youth, anxiety among our elderly, and there's virtual despair among the many who look beyond material success toward the inner meaning of their lives. The growing menace in our country tonight, to personal safety, to life, to limb and property, in homes, in churches, on the playgrounds and places of business, particularly in our great cities, is the mounting concern—or should be—of every thoughtful citizen in the United States. Security from domestic violence, no less than from foreign aggression, is the most elementary and fundamental purpose of any government, and a government that cannot fulfill this purpose cannot long command the loyalty of its citizens.

History demonstrates that nothing prepares the way of tyranny more than the failure of public officials to keep the streets safe from bullies and marauders.

We Republicans see in our constitutional form of government the great framework which assures the orderly but dynamic fulfillment of the whole man, and we see the whole man as the great reason for instituting orderly government in the first place. We see in the sanctity of private property the only durable foundation for constitutional government in a free society.

Anyone who joins us in all sincerity, we welcome. Those who do not care for our cause, we don't expect to enter our ranks in any case. And let our Republicanism, so focused and so dedicated, not be made fuzzy and futile by unthinking and stupid labels.

I would remind you that extremism in the defense of liberty is no vice!

And let me remind you also that moderation in the pursuit of justice is no virtue!

This Party, its good people, and its unquestionable devotion to freedom will not fulfill the purposes of this campaign which we launch here now until our cause has won the day, inspired the world, and shown the way to a tomorrow worthy of all our yesteryears.

Although some Republicans leave the hall as Sen. Goldwater ends his acceptance speech, the Convention roars its approval of the candidate, and the delegates join in singing "America The Beautiful."

McGEE: Republican moderates, their public face aside, are sad and dispirited. Gov. Scranton indicates that his Presidential ambitions have been permanently crushed. Looking four years ahead, Scranton said today, "I will have been out of office then for more than a year, and if you don't have a platform from which to run, you don't

have much of a chance." Gov. Rockefeller, according to NBC's Merrill Mueller, will do little or no active campaigning for the Miller-Goldwater ticket. He will concentrate on Senate and local legislative contests in New York. He will not be asked to the platform in the usual gesture of unity.

Today, former President Eisenhower spoke of the role that he expects to play in the campaign.

QUESTION: General, if Sen. Goldwater should ask you to actively participate in the campaign, are you willing to do so?

EISENHOWER: Well, now, let's don't start "iffing." Let's wait and see what they want to do. After all, you people mustn't forget I am a little bit older than when I started campaigning way back in '52, and so let's take it easy. Don't start pushing me.

QUESTION: General, last night you issued a statement. Could you tell us its substance?

EISENHOWER: I said I congratulate Sen. Goldwater upon the winning of the Republican nomination, and I applauded the action of Gov. Scranton for moving so promptly in an attempt to unify the Party, and I thought that his action, which was courageous, would be helpful in the November election. That's about it.

BRINKLEY: The Convention is now adjourned. I think it is not much of an overstatement to say that, on the whole, the Goldwater conservative Republican movement—and the Convention itself—have been a protest against the East. Sen. Goldwater once said jokingly that it might be a nice idea to saw loose the East Coast of the United States and let it float out to sea.

There were many significant developments that occurred here, and one especially deserves mention. This week, the souvenir hawkers were around San Francisco selling balloons, mechanical monkeys, pennants and buttons. Among the buttons, one of the most popular — a sellout in fact — was this one: "STAMP OUT HUNTLEY-BRINKLEY."

We all thought it was a joke, and we still do, but we find that most of those buying and wearing the buttons were serious, and they meant it. That, of course, is unimportant, except as it typifies the attitude of many of the Goldwater people at the Convention. They are belligerently crying that the press and television are unfair to their side, and are in some kind of unholy conspiracy against their man. In practice, it reached the ugly and primitive level of shoving and shouting in hotel lobbies, and insults spoken in elevators.

It is a little late in the history of literate society to have to explain that a reporter is not a cheer leader. His first responsibility is to those who read or listen to the news, and to nobody else. Here on the floor, the Republicans on one night voted to approve the Birch Society's and the Ku Klux Klan's right to dissent, but there was great anger because the press exercised the same right. All of the responsible elements in the press and in broadcasting will nevertheless go on doing what they have been doing—reporting the Republican and the Democratic campaigns fairly.

BRINKLEY: John Chancellor and Edwin Newman summarize their views of this Convention.

CHANCELLOR: What we've all been watching, of course, is a seizure of power, a kind of coup. It's been peaceful and legal and done completely in the open. I have been prowling the back aisles here, talking with Southern delegates who have for many years been largely ignored by the Republican Party. This year they managed to achieve a platform which was less strong on civil rights than the one written four years ago. They were delighted. And they've gone home filled with the sort of elation that has not been in that wing of the Party for many years.

I've also noted that both the winners and the losers here in the Convention were surprised. The winners were surprised because they'd been working for only four years to seize power in the Republican Party, and they didn't think they could do it that quickly. Yet they did. The losers were surprised for the same reason. Only four years ago they were firmly in control of the Republican Party—and tonight they were no longer in control.

NEWMAN: Sen. Goldwater's speech tonight did not bring into the fold those who were inclined to

95

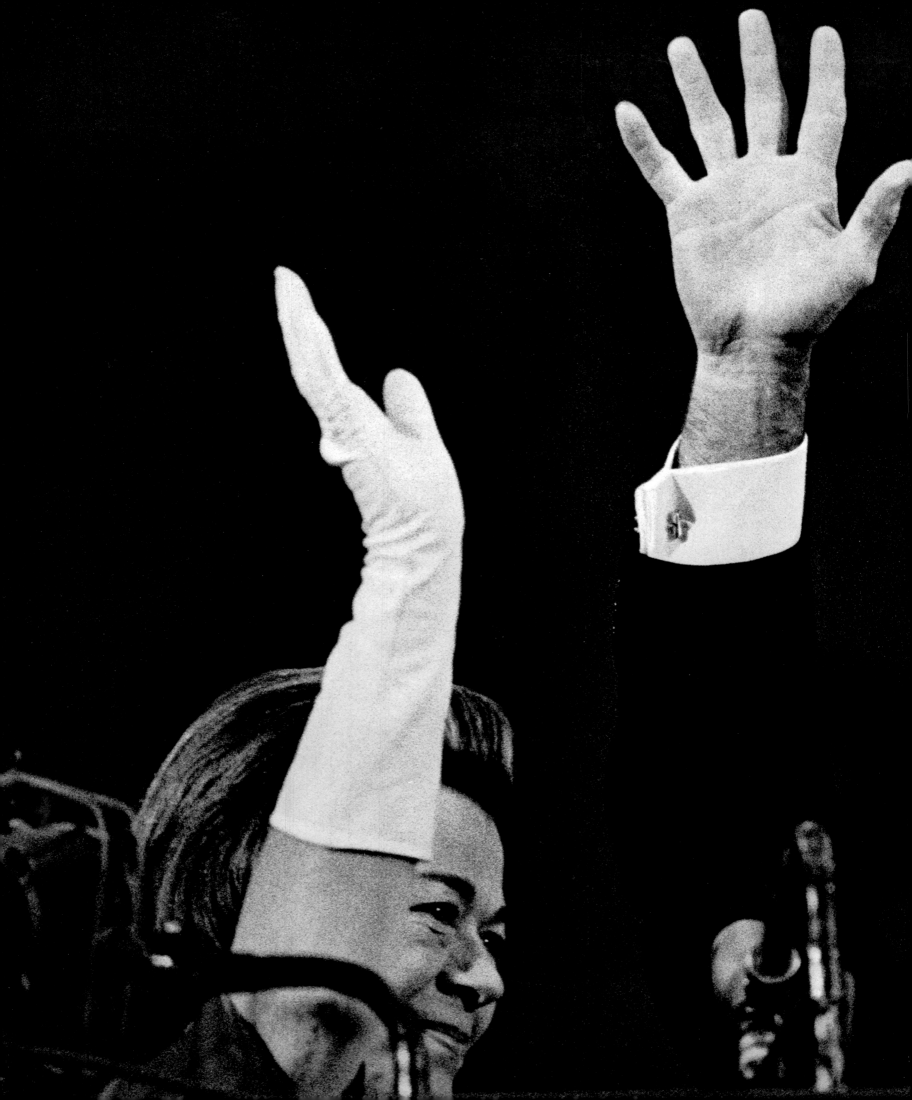

be outside before. The Maryland Negro delegates walked out—said they'd work against Goldwater in November. Gov. Chaffee of Rhode Island issued a very angry statement emphasizing his independence. A member of one delegation told me that in his delegation and in Vermont he'd heard talk to the effect "that Goldwater was not merely irresponsible but dangerous."

On the other hand, a number of Southern delegates have said that a great step has been taken towards establishing the two-Party system in the South. This has been an uncomfortable Convention because it sets up a fundamental political struggle in this country, and fundamental political struggles are not entirely compatible with the two-Party system.

It's been said in another connection that this is going to be a hot summer. It may be a long, hot political summer, too.

AN AFTERVIEW

How did Sen. Goldwater win the Republican Presidential nomination? Several weeks before the Convention in San Francisco, NBC talked with the Senator and his aides about their strategy for gaining the Party's nomination, with the understanding that nothing of what they revealed would be broadcast until after the Convention. On July 30, NBC News told the story.

GOLDWATER: The "Draft Goldwater" movement got started and I sort of laughed at it. I said, "Well, let them go ahead and do it. It's not going any place. At least they'll work off some steam." And when it became evident that there was interest—along about in October, 1963—I thought that possibly I should do it. Then President Kennedy was assassinated in November and I lost all interest. It was about four or five days later that I told my wife "to heck with the Presidential thing."

Kennedy was a liberal, a true liberal, and he always stayed that way. We used to argue about it. He used to come over [on the Senate floor] and say, "I saw you wince when I voted that time." I'd say, "Well, why the devil did you do it? Your father

would spank you." He said, "I just feel that way."

MacNEIL: Did Mr. Kennedy ever quietly indicate to you whether he thought it would be a good idea for you to run for the Presidency?

GOLDWATER: No, not exactly that way. The only thing I remember was the day of the Bay of Pigs. I won't use the exact words, but he called me. I went down and he was out of his office, but his girl said, "Go on in and sit down." So I went in and sat in his rocking chair. I forget whether I did it as a test—because we both used the same doctor, who was also trying to get me to get a rocker, but I didn't want one. And the President came in smoking that little cigar and he looked at me and he said, "Do you want this job?" I said, "No, not in my right mind." So he said, "I thought I had a good thing going—up to this point."

MacNEIL: In December, after you'd recovered from the Kennedy assassination, who was with you when you actually made the decision to run?

GOLDWATER: Oh, just me. I think I was probably sitting at my desk in my den. That's where I spend most of my time. I just finally said to myself, "You've got to do it." I realized that I had a responsibility to conservatism and to the young people who had become interested in it. I felt, too, that if I didn't do it, these young people (many of them voting for the first time), might drift away. I had a question in my mind all through the year, whether or not this was the right time for a conservative candidate to offer himself. I felt if he were clobbered at the Convention, or didn't even reach the Convention, that would be the end of conservatism in the Party. Or, if he were clobbered in the general election, that would write off conservatism in this country.

And frankly, I wasn't convinced that this was the year. But the more it goes along, the more I'm convinced that it is the year, and the decision was the right one, even though at the time I made it, it was a rather reluctant one.

MacNEIL: Can you remember whom you told first?

GOLDWATER: My wife, but I didn't tell her. I said, "Honey, what do you think about my running for the Presidency?" "Well," she said, "if that's what

you want to do, you go ahead and do it. I don't particularly want you to, but I'm not going to stand in your way." The only one who really raised particular Cain was my mother. She said she didn't want me being President. She wanted me in the Senate—probably because she felt she could see more of me.

MacNEIL: The real work of corralling delegates began. Richard Kleindienst [a top Goldwater aide] tells how their technique worked:

KLEINDIENST: One of the great miracles in American politics is the fact that between January and February 16, we had a Goldwater chairman in 46 out of 50 States, and a finance committee functioning in 25 or 30 States. We had regional directors, a research department, public information and public relations departments, and a staff in Washington. In six weeks we had put together this organization for Sen. Goldwater.

Then, let's say that a State convention was May 10. We had charts chronologically worked out so that maybe two or three months in advance we would have our initial correspondence with our State chairman. We would try to get from him a preliminary estimate of our getting delegates. We would then suggest to him that the precinct committeemen and county chairmen start urging the collection of delegates friendly to Sen. Goldwater. Two or three weeks prior to that convention, we would revisit the State chairman and go through the mechanics and details of a political convention. Who's going to be chairman of the nominating committee, the resolutions committee, the credentials committee? What arrangements have you made to be sure that the delegates who have been elected at the grass roots level are going to be present, or be represented by proxy at that convention? What is your strategy with respect to the composition of the delegation? Are we going to have a floor fight? If we have a floor fight, are you organized for it? If not, what can we do to get a resolution passed by this State convention committing the delegates in advance to the candidacy of Sen. Goldwater?

On the day of the State convention, either Clifford White [an early Goldwater leader] or myself, together with our regional directors, would be there. In most instances, we would request the right to speak to the delegates on behalf of our candidate. We would have caucuses in the back rooms of the hotels with our key leaders, devising our strategy. We would bring campaign materials, issue statements, buttons, bumper stickers. We would hope to have placards and signs made. One thing that I observed—while we were doing this, there was no other similar organization at these conventions on an effective basis.

MacNEIL: Joshua may have brought down the walls of Jericho just by using trumpets, but that's not a very reliable way to plan a battle. Yet, that's just what a lot of Republicans did this year. They blew their trumpets and waited for the walls to come tumbling down. While they were waiting, Barry Goldwater was busily engaged in digging holes and getting through. When the walls did come down, he had captured all the people inside.

CAPTIONS

THE DEMOCRATIC CONVENTION

W hen the Democratic Convention opens in Atlantic City, New Jersey, on Monday, August 24, Lyndon B. Johnson will be nominated for the Presidency. That much is certain. But who will be his Vice Presidential running mate? For months, speculation has included virtually every prominent Democrat. Some of the Party's most influential leaders openly endorse Attorney General Robert Kennedy, and NBC's Nancy Dickerson reports that Mrs. Jacqueline Kennedy will return from Europe to "help Bobby." Moreover, it is thought that a film tribute to the late President Kennedy, scheduled for the first night, might set off a wave of emotion that could sweep his younger brother onto the ticket. The speculation about the Attorney General's Vice Presidential possibilities ends on July 30 when Mr. Johnson announces that he is disqualifying "any member of my Cabinet or any of those who meet regularly with the Cabinet." Democratic Convention officials also arrange to have the John F. Kennedy tribute shifted to the last session, when all nominations will have been completed. Once the Attorney General is eliminated from the race, informed opinion picks Sen. Hubert Humphrey of Minnesota as the most likely choice. But the President plays the suspense for all it is worth, and as the Convention approaches, the Vice Presidential candidate's identity is still unknown.

The President is also busy on other fronts. On May 22, at the University of Michigan, he had outlined his "Great Society" theme. Now, he coins the word "frontlash," to describe Republicans who, he predicts, will vote the Democratic ticket out of dissatisfaction with Sen. Goldwater. On Aug. 4, he wins the nation's approval by ordering military retaliation against "certain facilities" in North Vietnam after American ships have been attacked in the Gulf of Tonkin. And he wins an important domestic victory on Aug. 8 when his anti-poverty legislation (voted against by Sen. Goldwater) is passed in Congress by an impressive margin. To top it off, public opinion polls show Mr. Johnson outdistancing Sen. Goldwater by almost three-to-one. The President is confident and in high spirits as the Democratic National Convention begins.

FIRST SESSION, AUGUST 24

HUNTLEY: This Convention is the supreme executive body of the Democratic Party. It makes the rules, and it is met here to do a number of things: nominate candidates for President and Vice President; adopt a platform, which will also serve as rebuttal against the slings and arrows of the opposition Party; elect a new National Committee

to manage the affairs of the Party between the end of this Convention and the beginning of the next one; and make whatever other regulations it thinks may advance its popularity and secure the loyalty and affection of the American voter.

Throughout the history of the Party, Democrats have fought among themselves. In times past, the quarrels concerned gold vs. silver, agriculture, tariffs and trade. But since 1948, the substance of Democratic fighting has shifted to civil rights and the broader issue of the South's role in national affairs. That issue is present here. Specifically, it concerns the seating of the Mississippi and Alabama delegations. Can this Democratic Party continue to accommodate the voters of the South? That question has bedeviled Democratic Conventions since 1948. And can Southerners find comfort under the Republican umbrella? That's the question which seized the Republican Convention this year, as well. This Democratic Convention may not resolve the question completely, but it may find a compromise.

---

*T*he Democrats find themselves fighting even before the first session begins. The fight centers on a dispute over the credentials of the Alabama and Mississippi delegations, which are clearly anti-Johnson. The day preceding the Convention, the Credentials Committee demanded that the Alabama dissidents sign a pledge binding them to support the ticket.

An overwhelming majority of the Alabama delegation refuse to comply. The Mississippi situation is complicated by the arrival in Atlantic City of a Mississippi group calling itself the Freedom Democrats. Its membership is primarily Negro, and it charges that the "regular" delegation is illegal because Negroes have been barred from the Mississippi Democratic Party. All day Sunday and Monday, a group of Democratic leaders, including Sen. Humphrey and Minnesota Attorney General Walter Mondale, seek to find a compromise on the Mississippi situation.

Outside the Convention Hall, civil rights pickets compete for attention with a contingent of uniformed members of the American Nazi Party. This latter group runs afoul of the Atlantic City police and is dispersed.

BRINKLEY: In all this talk about the seating or not seating of delegations, one thing worth remem-

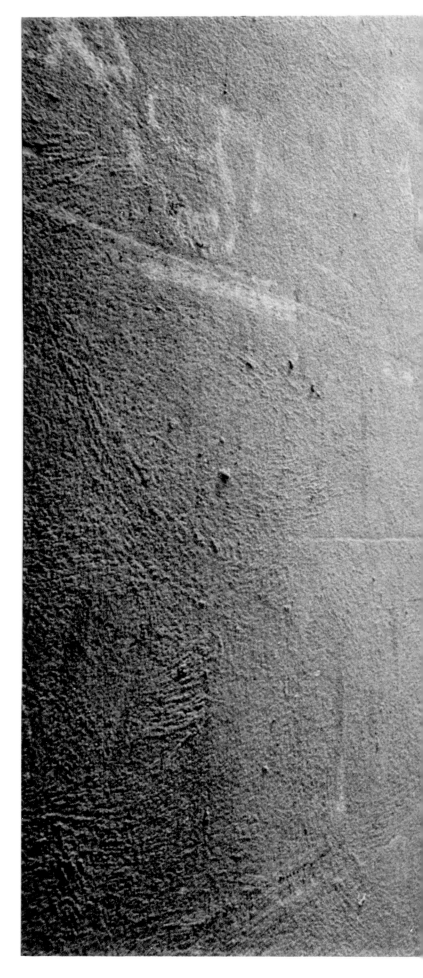

bering is that a Convention is totally sovereign in these matters. It cannot be taken into court; it cannot be questioned anywhere else. The courts have consistently refused to get into political arguments. So, when the Convention decides who is to be seated, there is no challenge.

An official of the Democratic Party in Mississippi was talking about this when he said, "The Convention could seat a dozen dead dodoes brought to Atlantic City in silver boxes and nobody could do anything about it." And he's quite right; nobody could.

Otherwise, the Democrats, with President Johnson in remote control from Washington, are trying their best to have a nice, quiet, peaceful Convention with a platform that will antagonize no one—or at most a minimum number of people.

With the first session called to order, the Convention's formalities get under way at the rostrum. Gov. Richard Hughes of New Jersey delivers his Address of Welcome, and there are speeches by the President of the Young Democratic Clubs of America and by the winner of this year's American Legion oratorical contest. Former Gov. David Lawrence of Pennsylvania, Chairman of the Credentials Committee, tells the delegates that his Committee is not ready with a report dealing with the Mississippi delegation. The Alabama delegates, meanwhile, take their seats, despite the fact that the majority have refused to sign the loyalty pledge.

The highlight of the first session is the fiery Keynote Address by Senator John O. Pastore of Rhode Island—the shortest member of the Senate from the smallest State. His speech is a virtuoso example of old-time oratory—complete with fist-pounding and finger-pointing—and it earns the Senator an ovation.

HIGHLIGHTS FROM SEN. PASTORE'S ADDRESS

I am a native American of immigrant parents who came to this great land at the turn of the century... My cup tonight runneth over, and the best way that I can express it is to say God Bless America!

We meet here tonight to assure the people of the United States and the people of the world that, on the American political scene, reason and respect and responsibility still survive.

Never before in the history of this great Republic have we known such prosperity. Moreover, in the process, we have built the mightiest military machine in the world. But, in the words of President Johnson, we maintain this power not for plunder, not for conquest, but in order to avoid conflict and in order to maintain peace.

When I hear anyone talk glibly and loosely about whose finger should be on the trigger, I become concerned. And I become concerned when people talk about who should make the decision; for in an all-out atomic war, there won't be any winner. The sanity of America is the security of the world.

And now they [the Republicans] profess to give a clear choice to the American people. Oh, what a Trojan horse! What is this clear choice? Do they mean the choice to renounce the nuclear test ban treaty? Do they mean to change our Social Security system? Do they mean to repeal the minimum wage law? Do they mean to weaken the unions in America? Do they mean we should withdraw from the Atlantic Alliance? Do they mean we should withdraw from the United Nations? Do they mean to turn the clock back 32 years and take away from the American people all these hard won social reforms?

We invite every American—Democrat, Independent and moderate Republican—to march forward with us in a more perfect union that is our American ideal.

With the full sincerity of my soul, I say that God did bless America on that day four years ago in Los Angeles when John F. Kennedy said, "I need you, Lyndon Johnson." And on Nov. 3, the American people will echo that call: "We need you, President Johnson."

The fight over the Alabama and Mississippi delegations continues. It is a fight that will result in a Convention decision of far-reaching consequences to the future of the Democratic Party. Two of the memorable moments of that controversy occur when Frank McGee, on the Convention floor, talks with two Alabama delegates.

McGEE: I'm down here in the Alabama delegation

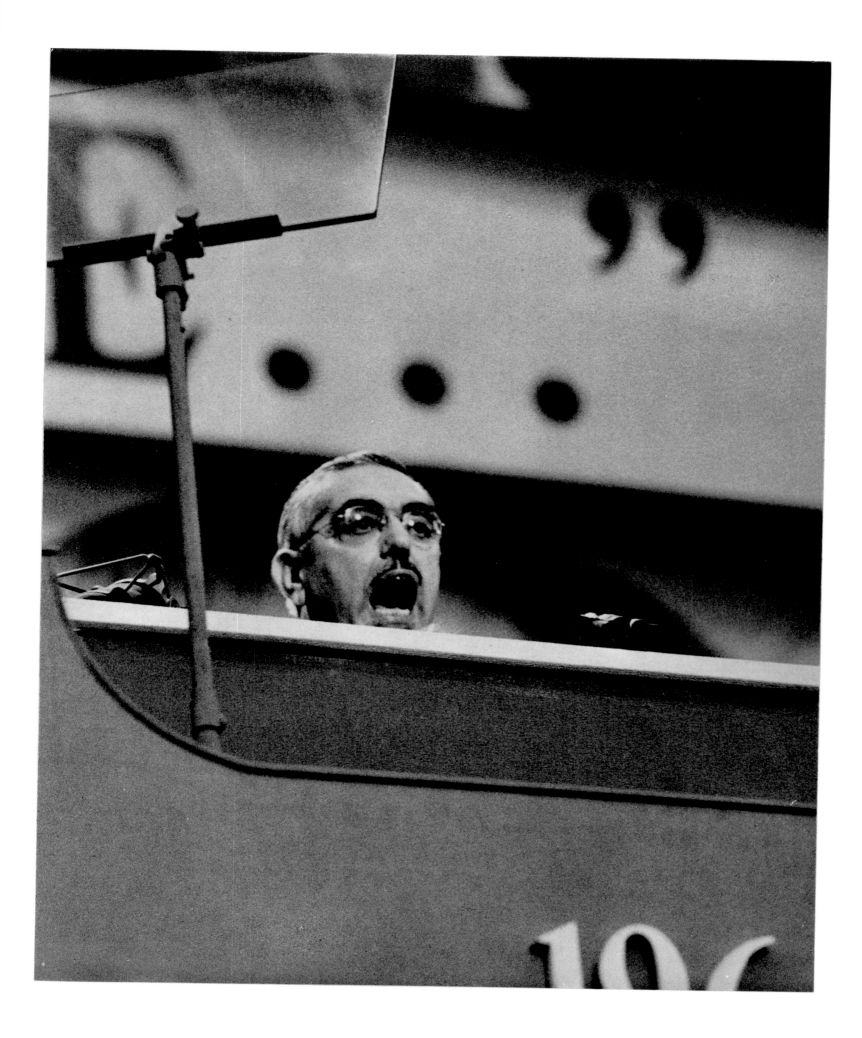

with Eugene "Bull" Connor of Birmingham. Sir, are you going to sign the loyalty pledge?

CONNOR: No, Sir. I said I would never sign a loyalty pledge tonight unless every delegate in America signed it here tonight.

McGEE: Are you going to sit in the delegation? What happens if they ask you to leave?

CONNOR: If they ask me to get out of the hall, I'll leave. I'll walk out like a gentleman.

BRINKLEY: The Alabama delegates were asked to do all they could, by lawful and honorable means, to persuade their unpledged Electors to vote for the Democratic Party nominee. Some Alabama delegates have agreed to sign the pledge, and in fact have signed it. Others have refused and have been told they may not be seated. But they have said they're going to stay, anyway.

McGEE: I am with Judge Roy McCord, of the Alabama delegation. Judge McCord, you signed the oath and were seated. Delegates who did not sign the oath nevertheless sat in the chairs. Do you think delegates who didn't take the pledge should give up their seats?

McCORD: I'm certainly not going to be a party to making any man or woman from Alabama give up a seat. I'm not going to be a party to running any of my friends off this Convention floor.

McGEE: Is it possible, Sir, that this situation can continue throughout the Convention—that those of you who signed the oath will sit here and those who did not sign the oath will also sit here?

McCORD: That would be possible. I certainly will do nothing to run any of these good Democrats that came up here out of the seats that they got or the seats that they want to sit in. They're my friends. I got to go back home and live with them. I love some of them. I think they're wrong. They don't seem to see it right. They think that it's casting aspersions upon their honor and integrity. I don't go along with that idea. But I admire their courage. I say they are good men, and I certainly would not run them out of the Democratic Party.

McGEE: You have not been out of this chair all

night long. Is there some reason for your being so careful not to get up from this seat?

McCORD: Well, I like this seat. It's pretty good. [Laughter] You know, I went over every hill and holler and dale and crossed every bridge in the 5th Congressional District — eight big counties — to get that seat. And I don't want nobody—friend or foe—to take it away from me.

McGEE: You think there's a possibility somebody might grab it if you left it for a minute?

McCORD: I wouldn't be a bit surprised.

BRINKLEY: Chet, I cast one non-partisan vote for Judge Roy McCord of Alabama. He is not going to abandon his friends. He thinks they are wrong, that they are misguided, but he is not going to abandon them, whatever happens.

With the formal acceptance of the rules of order for this Convention, the first session ends. Still unresolved are the seating of the disputed Mississippi delegations and the identity of the Democratic Party's Vice Presidential candidate.

HUNTLEY: This serial will continue tomorrow, perhaps with answers to several breathless questions: Will the Alabama delegation take a pledge to the Democratic Party? If the delegation members refuse, will they walk out? Will they be forced out? Will they be invited to leave? Will they be carried out? Or will they just be left seated without a vote?

BRINKLEY: Will the Alabama delegation find happiness on Atlantic City's sunswept shores?

HUNTLEY: And will Hubert Humphrey be the Vice Presidential nominee?

BRINKLEY: Tune in tomorrow.

SECOND SESSION, AUGUST 25

This evening, the delegates will hear speeches by Rep. John W. McCormack of Massachusetts, Speaker of the House, who is the Permanent Chairman of the Convention, and by Sen. Birch Bayh of Indiana. There will also be the inevitable reading of the entire platform. But the principal interest continues to center on the seating of those Southern delegations.

BRINKLEY: When we left the Convention last night, the question of seating the delegations from Alabama and Mississippi was unresolved.

Late this afternoon, the Credentials Committee finally came up with what it regarded as a fair compromise. In essence, it asked that the Convention "welcome as honored guests" the members of the delegation of the Freedom Democratic Party, and that two Freedom delegates "be afforded full delegate status in a special category of delegates-at-large." Further, the Committee recommended that in 1968, voters should be assured of a chance to take part in State Party affairs "regardless of race, color, creed, or national origin."

A few minutes after this session was called to order, the Convention overwhelmingly approved this compromise. But both the Regular Democrats and the Freedom Democrats rejected it, and most of the Regular Mississippi delegation has withdrawn from the Convention. So, tonight nothing is settled.

HUNTLEY: What to do about the Alabama and Mississippi delegations plagues this Convention. Tom Pettit and Edwin Newman report.

PETTIT: Alabama is sending two delegations to the Convention floor tonight. The loyalist faction claims 13 members, Roy McCord and Rubin Newton as co-chairmen. These people have signed the so-called "loyalty pledge" and they intend to represent Alabama.

However, the Regular delegation — those who refused to sign the pledge — late today said they would also go to the Convention floor. This faction includes Eugene "Bull" Connor. There still is a hotel suite here reserved for Gov. Wallace, although he is in Alabama. It is widely accepted that he is exercising wide influence over those delegates who refuse to sign the loyalty pledge and who are going to the floor tonight.

NEWMAN: The recommendation of the Credentials Committee to solve the problem of a Mississippi delegation rested on one key point. That was that the Freedom Democratic Party (the largely Negro group) be given two delegates to

the Convention—not delegates from Mississippi, but delegates-at-large. Before this offer was made, the Credentials Committee was unable to put forward any settlement that would not have meant a floor fight. The Johnson administration wanted to avoid a floor fight. The offer of the two delegates-at-large was taken as a way out. Three points had been agreed on before this.

First, that the Regular Mississippi delegates be seated if they promise to be loyal in November.

Second, that in future Conventions, delegations would be seated only if they came from State Parties open to all without regard to color.

Third, that the Democratic National Committee would help State Democratic Parties to meet that requirement and report on whether they had.

All these, the Convention accepted by its vote. But those three points have left the Freedom Democratic Party with no place in the Convention except as honored guests. That would have meant a floor fight to get the two delegations treated equally. Then, with Sen. Humphrey working behind the scenes with Attorney General Walter Mondale of Minnesota, Chairman of the Credentials Sub-Committee, another offer was made.

It was a proposal that two seats go to Aaron Henry, a druggist who is Chairman of the Freedom delegation, and Mississippi Chairman of the NAACP; and to the Rev. Edwin King, a white man, who's Chaplain of Tougaloo College in Jackson, which has a predominantly Negro student body.

The theory behind the offer was that it could be represented as a victory for the Freedom delegation. Walter Mondale called it a great breakthrough for civil rights. At the same time, the two delegates were not to be subtracted from the Regular Mississippi seats, and they were not to sit together. Also, the Mississippi all-white people were to be soothed by the Credentials Committee, saying that the Negro group was not really a political party, but a protest movement. That left the Regulars legally in possession of the field.

While both the contesting Mississippi factions have rejected the proposal, the two members of the Mississippi Freedom delegation accepted their "at-large" status, entered the hall and were seated with the Alaska delegation.

HUNTLEY: We have several times heard reference to a statement made today by Gov. Johnson of the State of Mississippi concerning the seating of this Mississippi delegation. Here it is:

GOV. JOHNSON: This man, Joseph Demagogue Rauh [legal adviser to Freedom Democrats], made statements about Mississippi that would be enough to make any ordinary back-alley degenerate ashamed of himself. I want to say to the people of America that these statements that this man Rauh made about my State and about the people of this State and about the leaders down through history and about me, were vicious, malicious, pusillanimous, premeditated, plain, ordinary, bald-faced, self-made, contemptible, abominable, self-concocted lies.

The responsible people and those knowledgeable people of America and those from every State in the Union who have visited our State, know that these statements were untrue. I am informed by leaders of the Mississippi delegation to the National Democratic Convention that Mississippi's legally constituted delegation would be seated only if the individual members thereof would sign a loyalty oath.

I am further informed that the entire Mississippi delegation, perhaps with the exception of two or three, flatly refuses to take any such oath, and I am proud of them for their courageous stand. Never before in the history of any political party have individual delegates been required to take loyalty oaths simply because a handful of dissident, non-resident troublemakers saw fit to challenge a legal delegation. If this had been a requirement in 1960, Lyndon Baines Johnson would not today be President of the United States. This action by the Credentials Committee means that our entire delegation, with these few exceptions mentioned, will not participate in any way in the affairs and actions of the National Democratic Convention. The requirement of a loyalty oath was a device to take the Democratic Party off the

115

spot so they would not have to face up to a choice between Mississippi's legal delegation, and a handful of professional Negro extremists.

BRINKLEY: One of Mr. Rauh's charges was that Mississippi's Negroes were not allowed to participate in the Party's activities. His other charge was that the Regulars are not loyal to the Party and are very likely to go back to Mississippi and vote for Sen. Goldwater. Democrats may find this charge regrettable, but it is not illegal.

KAPLOW: One of the perplexities assailing this Convention is that there are grave doubts that the Mississippi Freedom delegation is legally constituted. The fact is that if it did not fulfill the State laws and requirements of Mississippi, this Convention can't seat it.

And on the other hand, the Regular Mississippi Democratic delegation, no matter what sins it may have committed, seems to be legally constituted, and it seems to have fulfilled the requirements of the laws in the State of Mississippi.

HUNTLEY: The Convention has now amended the rules for the 1968 Convention. It is demanding the right of Negroes to participate in all levels of the Democratic Party in the South. A commission has been established to watch developments in the South and to see if Negroes are given an opportunity to participate in the Democratic Party.

That rule is sure to cause political charges and counter-charges, and it will probably bring about political changes throughout the South.

CHANCELLOR: I'm outside the hall, in the middle of the Mississippi Freedom Democratic Party. They say all 68 or 69 delegates are here. They're starting to march on Convention Hall now. There's a great crush of press and delegates and onlookers here, and the delegation is very slowly making its way across the boardwalk behind a phalanx of young men, white and colored, who have linked their arms to precede Dr. Henry [Chairman, the Freedom Democratic delegation].

They're heading toward the northeast corner

117

of the hall, which is one of the entrances. Dr. Henry now has tickets. Dr. Henry, can you tell me what it says on the ticket?

HENRY: VIP. Very Important Person.

CHANCELLOR: It says "VIP Alternate." Do you know where that will allow you to sit?

HENRY: Man, I don't know. We'll find out when we get inside.

CHANCELLOR: Why are you marching?

HENRY: The same reason the other delegates are inside. We came to this Convention to be a part of it, and we're still trying to be a part of it.

CHANCELLOR: You refused the offer of the Credentials Committee today to allow two of you in as full delegates with voting privileges.

HENRY: That didn't give us status as Mississippi people. That was an "at-large" situation.

CHANCELLOR: They're all pushing, and the police here have stopped them. Apparently some kind of conference is going on. James Foreman [of the Student Non-Violent Coordinating Committee] is arguing the case, and the police here are standing firm. The police have told James Foreman that there is no more space in the hall. He said nobody else can get in there, not even reporters. The impasse in the Credentials Committee has been moved to the impasse at the northeast corner of the boardwalk. Ironically, this is taking place on Mississippi Avenue. The Freedom Democratic Party is in its last stand.

BRINKLEY: I don't know what instructions the police have, and I don't want to argue with them, but as for there being no more room in the hall, that isn't true. There is. There are quite a number of empty seats—in the alternate section, some in the delegate section, and some in the VIP section.

The Regular Mississippi delegation has declined to take any further part in the Convention, and presumably they are going home. The Freedom Democratic Party is at the front gates, trying to get in, and apparently cannot.

HUNTLEY: Sen. Humphrey blamed the non-acceptance of the Mississippi compromise on extremists —as indeed there have been extreme opinions on both sides. This debate has agonized delegations and it agonizes the entire Convention. But the fact is the Humphrey compromise has been accepted by the Convention-at-large, including most of the Southern delegations, as well as those supporting the Mississippi Freedom Party.

SCHERER: Sen. Humphrey, who labored on the Mississippi compromise, feels that a good deal was accomplished. Here's the Senator now.

[To Humphrey] Since neither party agreed to the compromise, it's been interpreted as a setback. What do you think you accomplished?

HUMPHREY: This was a very good victory for the Democratic Party. The Party overwhelmingly accepted this resolution of the Credentials Committee. It was a victory for the forces of reason.

BRINKLEY: This will be platform night—the night when the Democrats present their program to the Convention. We've looked it over and we find that the classic and traditional habit of platform writers—of appealing to as many groups of people as possible—has been followed by the Democrats to a degree not often matched.

In skimming through it, we see that the Party offers to do good for the following groups: immigrants, babies, grandmothers, women, older people looking for jobs, the poor, labor union members, the handicapped, businessmen, retired people, white people, Negroes and Indians.

The 22,000-word Democratic Party platform is read to the delegates (although not all remain in the hall to hear it), by a relay of Democratic candidates for office from across the country. In comments broadcast during the preparation of the Democratic platform before the Convention opened (NBC-TV's CAMPAIGN AND THE CANDIDATES—*August 23, 1964), Frank McGee reported.*

McGEE: Comparing the Republican and Democratic platforms, one could be forgiven for concluding that they don't refer to the same country at all. The most glaring contrast in the two platforms, so far, concerns control of nuclear weapons. Because Republican moderates lost their fight, the GOP platform says nothing on that question. Sen.

Goldwater's belief that the NATO Commander should be given some authority over tactical nuclear weapons remains the Party's policy. The Democratic platform states flatly: "Control of the use of nuclear weapons must remain solely with the highest elected official in the country, the President of the United States."

BRINKLEY: The reading of the platform continues. There are only two planks that are surprising. The one on civil rights includes this statement: "The Civil Rights Act of 1964 deserves and requires full observance by every American, and fair, effective enforcement if there is any default." The general interpretation here has been that this means the Federal government should enforce the civil rights law only when and where local or State jurisdictions fail to enforce the law.

The plank on extremism was written to contrast with the one not adopted by the Republicans. It says, "We must expose, wherever it exists, the advocacy of hatred which creates the clear and present danger of violence. We condemn extremism whether from the Right or Left, including the extreme tactics of such organizations as the Communist Party, the Ku Klux Klan, and the John Birch Society. We know what violence and hate can do. We have seen the tragic consequences of misguided zeal and twisted logic."

The platform is adopted by a voice vote, and the historic second session of the Democratic Convention comes to an end one minute before midnight.

THIRD SESSION, AUGUST 26

BRINKLEY: Tonight's Convention session should be extremely interesting. President Johnson will be nominated, and he will personally tell the delegates whom he wants to have for Vice President. It's never been done that way before. After Sen. Goldwater was nominated, he announced to a committee that his choice was Rep. William E. Miller. When this was passed around town, it reached the Tennessee delegation, where one of the delegates said, "William E. Who?"

On this day of August 26—mid-point in the Convention—speculation that Sen. Humphrey will be the Vice Presidential choice is widespread, the more so because this morning Sen. Eugene McCarthy, Humphrey's colleague from Minnesota, sent a telegram to the White House suggesting that the nomination go to Sen. Humphrey. Sen. McCarthy, an eloquent speaker, had come to national attention during the 1960 Democratic Convention with a moving nominating speech for Gov. Adlai Stevenson. The Senator is a close friend of President Johnson, and some insiders who like to bet on dark horses believed that he might get the nod.

This morning's telegram to the White House ends that abruptly. Newsman Robert Abernethy speaks with Sen. McCarthy very soon thereafter.

ABERNETHY: Were you told by the President that you would not be his running mate?

McCARTHY: That's right. He told me that he had read my telegram. That was about the extent of our conversation. He did not ask me to make the nominating speech, but I've had some conversation since with some other White House people about the possibility of some participation in the program tonight.

ABERNETHY: Why did you send your telegram?

McCARTHY: The Convention reaches a certain stage when it's not subject to any very rational analysis. You have to sense what the situation is and at that point, action is better than inaction.

ABERNETHY: In your telegram to the White House, you said you felt Mr. Humphrey met the qualifications the President laid down for the Vice Presidency. Does that mean you feel you don't fit these qualifications?

McCARTHY: What I said was that Sen. Humphrey met the qualifications that were laid down by President Johnson.

CHANCELLOR: The vigil held by members of CORE and SNCC in support of the Mississippi Freedom Democratic Party here on the boardwalk outside the Convention Hall is now in its 64th hour. This whole area has been crowded with demonstrators

and militants of various kinds, ranging from railroad firemen who are opposed to Public Law 88-108 (which requires compulsory arbitration), to a bagpipe band supporting Richard Daley, the Mayor of Chicago.

Earlier today, Dick Gregory, the Negro comedian who's often involved in these affairs, telegraphed the President demanding an amnesty for all people held in jails in the United States in connection with civil rights offenses — which, incidentally, the President is not empowered to grant.

HUNTLEY: Perhaps we can make one last supreme effort to explain what occurred at this Convention concerning the problem presented by political conviction, political organization, social custom, and the race question in the State of Mississippi. You have to start with certain facts.

One: the Democratic Party in Mississippi, like many of that State's institutions, has not been entirely open to Negroes.

Two: a white, duly elected, duly constituted delegation came to this Convention.

Three: another Mississippi delegation came — largely Negro. There are many doubts about its qualifications and whether or not it had met the requirements of the laws of the State of Mississippi governing political organization.

Four: the other—or Freedom—delegation said, "How can we meet the requirements of the laws when we are prevented from doing so, and when the laws themselves are sometimes unjust?"

Five: the Regular Democrats of Mississippi have not completed their State convention, and they may or may not put the nominees of this National Convention on their State ballot. They have warned that they will not support the national ticket. Their Electors in the Electoral College may not cast their votes for President Johnson, even if he should win in that State.

Six: the Freedom Democrats were pledged to support the national ticket. Therefore, question: Which delegation should this Convention seat?

Seven: testimony, some of it heartbreaking, was heard—and the debate ensued in the Credentials Committee. Due largely to the efforts of Walter Reuther, the labor leader, and Sen. Humphrey, a compromise was worked out. It would permit two Freedom Democrat delegates to be seated; the rest would be seated with no votes. The Regular Democrats would be required to take a pledge of loyalty to the Party, and promise to work for the nominees.

Eight: the Mississippi Regular Democrats refused the compromise last night.

Nine: the Freedom Democrats listened to the urgings of Mr. Reuther, Sen. Humphrey and their own leaders to accept it, to go back to Mississippi with something, with status, with acceptance. The Convention also established a committee to help Negroes participate in all levels of the Democratic Party within the next four years. That was part of the offer. But the Freedom group also turned down that proposition. And why? Well, some of them were simply unskilled and untrained in the art of political compromise. Some of them dreamed some excessive dreams of getting everything in one resolution or all on one ballot. Others wanted the case to come to the Convention floor, to see this Convention, in full glare of the nation, debate their cause and their case. A young and bright religious leader who has been working in Mississippi for several years was almost in tears last night. He said emotionalism had overcome restraint. He and others like him felt that somehow they had failed.

However, all perhaps was not lost. The two members of the Freedom delegation accepted by the Convention came in and took their seats. They had come the long distance. Other members of the Freedom group came in and sat in the Mississippi seats because the Regular delegation had left. There was some confusion for awhile. There were mixed signals, sergeants at arms tried to force them out, but finally it was decided they could stay.

That is the sequence of events.

What has been won or lost? What has been promised and committed? Where is this Democratic Party now on this agonizing question of civil rights and voter popularity in the South?

123

It's not entirely resolved. It won't be resolved, perhaps, for many years to come, but it certainly becomes apparent that the laws, rules, and resolutions of this Convention are not going to resolve it. Wisdom and restraint and talking it out are probably going to be the final weapons.

BRINKLEY: Down on the boardwalk a big billboard appeared advertising Goldwater. It showed a picture of him, with the legend: "Vote for Barry Goldwater. In your heart you know he is right." Some Democrats added immediately under it another small signboard, saying, "Yes, extreme Right." Late this afternoon the little addendum put up by the Democrats came down.

Perhaps whoever put up the billboard—we don't know who it was—also hired the airplane that flew over the beach this afternoon as Mrs. Johnson was arriving. The airplane's streamer proclaimed: "Bobby Baker for Vice President."

CHANCELLOR: There is something going on here in the south aisle of Convention Hall. Here's "Bull" Connor of the Alabama delegation. Mr. Connor, can you tell us what's happening here?
CONNOR: Let's get this straight, every one of you. I'm not leaving! They're taking me out!
CHANCELLOR: Who asked you to leave?
CONNOR: The sergeant at arms.
CHANCELLOR: Did he give any reason for it?
CONNOR: He said I had not signed a pledge.
CHANCELLOR [To camera]: I think you could all hear the testimony of Mr. Connor, who was thrown out. Other people here in this great crush are saying that he was not thrown out.
CONNOR: Get that microphone out of my eye! I'm not saying no more until I get out of here.
CHANCELLOR: That may be one of the more definitive statements of the Convention. He said it loud and clear. We're trying to clear a way so Mr. Connor can get down the aisle. Here is "Bull" Connor walking down the aisle of the Convention, saying he has been ordered to leave. He who came here to test his ability to remain seated in the Alabama delegation is now leaving the Convention Hall.

With the departure of the Alabama delegates who persist in their refusal to sign the loyalty pledge, the atmosphere in Convention Hall changes. At 8:18 pm of this third session, Mrs. Lady Bird Johnson and her daughters, Lynda and Luci, enter the hall. As the First Lady and her daughters proceed to the Presidential Box, a wild demonstration in their honor breaks loose on the floor—a demonstration with music and cheers that goes on for 25 minutes.

HUNTLEY: It becomes apparent that this is "good feeling" night at the Democratic National Convention. This is "happiness" night. The battles and struggles and clashes of the past few days will probably be put aside, and fade into something approaching oblivion. These delegates want to cheer. They want to applaud. They want to demonstrate, and tonight they're doing it.

This mood is to explode into an even more tumultuous demonstration when the President himself arrives at the Convention a short time afterward. The President announces in Washington during the afternoon that he would fly to Atlantic City to reveal his choice for the Vice Presidential nomination. But the suspense, which he so artistically (and sometimes even playfully) created during the months and days before the Convention, finally ends. During the afternoon the President asks Sen. Humphrey to fly from Atlantic City to the White House—and after the meeting, Sen. Humphrey and Sen. Dodd of Connecticut are invited to accompany him back to Atlantic City. Before leaving the capital, President Johnson refers to Sen. Humphrey as "the next Vice President"—and the secret is out.

During their flight North to Atlantic City, President Johnson, Sen. Humphrey and the others watch the Convention on airborne TV. They see the President himself being nominated by his longtime close friend and political associate, Gov. John B. Connally of Texas. There is drama in this selection of a nominator, for it was Gov. Connally who had been driving in the car with President Kennedy last November 22, and Gov. Connally himself had been gravely wounded. It was also Gov. Connally who had nominated Mr. Johnson for the Presidency in the unsuccessful bid in 1956. Addressing the Convention, Gov. Connally says that in the mournful hour of President Kennedy's death, "under the calm, firm leadership of Lyndon Johnson, we learned gratefully that we could survive not only personal loss, but national tragedy. Never in our history has any man come

125

to the Presidency better prepared or tested for the supreme task of leadership."

In a departure from Convention traditions, there is a "co-nominator," Gov. Edmund Brown of California. Gov. Brown praises President Johnson's "softspoken words of calm reason [which had] united and reassured people of every State and every section."

Mr. Johnson and the Presidential party land at the Atlantic City airport as Gov. Brown is speaking. A large crowd is on hand to greet the President, and the first correspondents to reach him as he steps off the plane are NBC's Nancy Dickerson and Ray Scherer, who interview him on television about his Vice Presidential choice. As the interview proceeds, other reporters join in the questioning.

NANCY DICKERSON: Hello, Mister President. How do you feel?

THE PRESIDENT: Fine. I'm so happy to see you. You've been doing wonderful; I've been watching.

NANCY DICKERSON: Mr. President, when did you make up your mind?

THE PRESIDENT: Oh, the middle of the afternoon.

NANCY DICKERSON: And then you told Sen. Humphrey as soon as you knew?

THE PRESIDENT: I was walking around the White House lawn with some of your colleagues and I thought it would be a good idea to ask the Senator to come down and talk to me about it. When I got back to the office I called him and he came down and we had a nice visit. We met with the Secretary of State and the Secretary of Defense and we exchanged viewpoints and made the decision.

SCHERER: Mr. President, how much campaigning are you going to assign to Sen. Humphrey?

THE PRESIDENT: All he can take.

SCHERER: How much would you say, Senator?

HUMPHREY: All he asks me to do.

QUESTION: What were some of the factors that went into your selection of Sen. Humphrey?

THE PRESIDENT: I thought the people of this country and the people of the free world were entitled to a man as Vice President . . . who would be the best-equipped man in this nation to be President, if something happened to the President.

He needed to be a person who was well versed in our relations with other nations. Sen. Hum-phrey is widely traveled, is very learned and has spent many years on the [Senate] Foreign Relations Committee, and is respected by our allies and our adversaries alike. I wanted a person that could go to any section of this country and talk about the problems of the people, and to give them leadership and compassion. I wanted a person who was familiar with the problems of Congress and had an understanding for the difficulties they labored under and could provide their leadership for them. I wanted youth and vigor, and vitality coupled with compassion and judgment and wisdom. And I considered many good and wise men, and I think I picked the best one.

QUESTION: May we ask the Senator what his reaction was when you gave him the word?

HUMPHREY: To put it concisely, I was both honored and almost overwhelmed. And I want to thank the President very much for his faith and confidence in me. And what he has said makes me humbly grateful and desirous of doing the very best that I can possibly do.

The nominating addresses for President Johnson are followed by seven seconding speeches. Then, the delegates nominate him by acclamation.

The President enters Convention Hall at 9:43 pm to a rousing demonstration by the delegates and spectators.

He then establishes a Convention precedent by his gaveling the delegates to order, and personally delivering what amounts to the nominating speech for Sen. Humphrey—a "man who" speech in which he does not mention the Senator by name until the final sentence, at which time he virtually shouts it.

The formal nominating speech is delivered by Sen. Humphrey's colleague from Minnesota, Sen. Eugene McCarthy, who had earlier sent the telegram to the President urging Humphrey's selection. Sen. Humphrey is also nominated by acclamation, but by now it is so late that his acceptance speech, originally scheduled for this night, is put off to the Convention's final session.

FOURTH SESSION, AUGUST 27

On the agenda are the acceptance speech of President Johnson, the acceptance speech by Sen. Hubert Humphrey (rescheduled from the preceding night), and films about President Johnson and President Kennedy. Before the long

final session ends, the delegates will have experienced one of the most emotionally charged nights in the history of political Conventions. At 8:21, the Convention sees "The Road to Leadership", a 28-minute documentary film about President Johnson. Then, the moment that everyone in the hall has been waiting for: the appearance of Robert F. Kennedy, who will be introducing "A Thousand Days," a filmed tribute to his late brother—John F. Kennedy. The Attorney General stands on the podium unable to speak for thirteen minutes, because of the unrelenting applause coming from the delegates below him.

HIGHLIGHTS FROM ROBERT F. KENNEDY'S ADDRESS

I first want to thank all of you delegates to this Democratic National Convention and the supporters of the Democratic Party for all that you did for President John F. Kennedy...

In all of [his] efforts, you were there. All of you. And when there were difficulties you sustained him. When there were periods of crisis, you stood beside him. When there were periods of happiness, you laughed with him. And when there were periods of sorrow, you comforted him.

I realize that as an individual we can't just look back, that we must look forward. When I think of President Kennedy I think of what Shakespeare said in ROMEO AND JULIET:
"When he shall die,
 Take him and cut him out in little stars,
 And he will make the face of heaven so fine
 That all the world will be in love with night,
 And pay no worship to the garish sun."
President Kennedy once said that we have the capacity to make this the best generation in the history of mankind, or make it the last. If we do our duty, if we meet our responsibilities, and our obligations, not just as Democrats but as American citizens in our local cities and towns and farms and in the country as a whole, then this generation is going to be the best generation in the history of mankind.

CHANCELLOR: We are told that President Johnson spent months before the Convention worrying about the effect of the appearance of Bobby Kennedy on the platform, wondering if it would

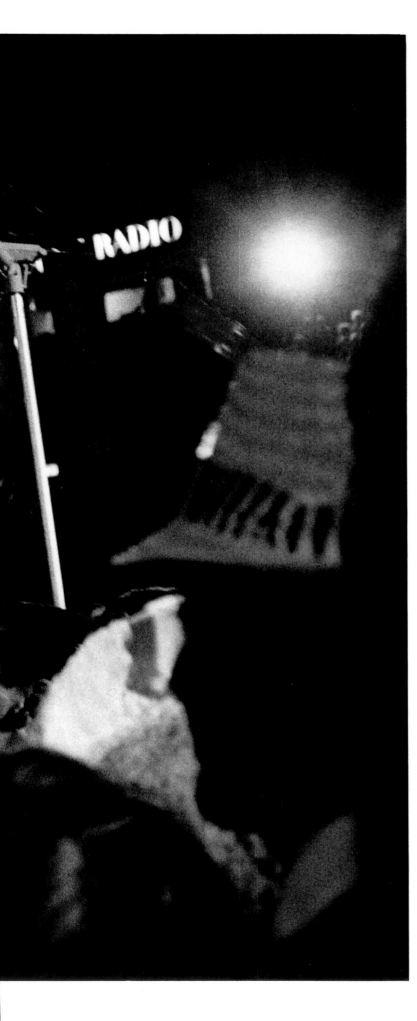

electrify and move the Convention. It electrified and moved the Convention tonight, but it was placed so late in the program that it wouldn't have altered the effects here. All the predictors who said Bobby's appearance here would change the mood and tempo of the Convention were absolutely right.

Robert Kennedy's appearance, and the poignant film about President Kennedy, are followed by tributes to the late Mrs. Eleanor Roosevelt by Ambassador Adlai Stevenson and to the late House Speaker Sam Rayburn by the Hon. James A. Farley. At the conclusion of these speeches, President Johnson enters the hall and joins Mrs. Johnson and Mr. and Mrs. Robert Kennedy in the Presidential Box. At 10:24, Sen. Humphrey begins his acceptance speech for the Vice Presidential nomination.

HIGHLIGHTS FROM SEN. HUMPHREY'S SPEECH

During the last few weeks, shrill voices have tried to lay claim to the great spirit of the American past, but they long for a past that never was. In their recklessness, in their irrationalism, they distort the American conservative tradition. Yes, those who have kidnapped the Republican Party have made it this year not a Party of memory and sentiment, but one of stridency, of unrestrained passion, of extreme and radical language.

The American Presidency is not a place for a man who is impetuous at one moment and indecisive the next. Nor is it a place for one who is violently for something one day and violently opposed to it on the next. Nor is this an office where statements on matters of major foreign policy are so confusing and so contradictory that neither friend nor foe knows where he stands. And it is of the highest importance that both friend and foe know that the American President means what he says and says what he means.

The temporary spokesman of the Republican Party—yes, the temporary spokesman—is not only out of tune with the great majority of his countrymen, he is even out of step with his own Party.

In the last three-and-a-half years most Democrats and Republicans have agreed on the great

decisions our nation has made. But not the Republican spokesman. Not Sen. Goldwater.

Most Democrats and Republicans in the United States voted for the nuclear test ban treaty, but not the temporary Republican spokesman.

Most Democrats and Republicans in the Senate voted for a tax cut for American citizens and American business, but not Sen. Goldwater.

Most Democrats and Republicans in the Senate —in fact, four-fifths of the members of his own Party—voted for the Civil Rights Act, but not Sen. Goldwater.

Most Democrats and Republicans in the Senate voted last year for an expanded medical-education program, but not Sen. Goldwater.

Most Democrats and Republicans in the Senate voted for the National Defense Education Act, but not the temporary Republican spokesman.

And, my fellow Americans, most Democrats and Republicans in the Senate voted to help the U. N. in its peace-keeping functions when it was in financial difficulties, but not Sen. Goldwater.

I say to those responsible and forward-looking Republicans who put our country above their Party—and there are thousands of them—we welcome you to the banner of Lyndon B. Johnson. We welcome your support...

Sen. Humphrey's speech is followed by the appearance on the podium of President Lyndon B. Johnson, who delivers his Acceptance Address.

HIGHLIGHTS FROM THE PRESIDENT'S SPEECH

My fellow Americans—I accept your nomination.

And I thank you, from the bottom of my heart, for placing at my side the man that last night you so wisely selected to be the next Vice President of the United States. The gladness of this high occasion cannot mask the sorrow which shares our hearts. So let us here tonight, each of us, all of us, rededicate ourselves to keeping burning the golden torch of promise which John Fitzgerald Kennedy set aflame.

Prosperity for most has not meant prosperity

for all. And those who have received the bounty of this land must not now turn from the needs of their neighbors.

Weapons do not make peace; man makes peace. And peace comes not through strength alone, but through wisdom and patience and restraint.

Every American has the right to be treated as a person. He should be able to find a job. He should be able to educate his children. He should be able to vote in elections. And he should be judged on his merits as a person. We cannot and we will not allow this great purpose to be endangered by reckless acts of violence. Those who break the law, those who create disorder, whether in the North or the South, must be brought to justice.

This nation, this generation, in this hour has man's first chance to build a great society, a place where the meaning of man's life matches the marvels of man's labor. I am determined in all the time that is mine to use all the talents that I have for bringing this great lovable land, this great nation of ours, together. I believe some day we will see an America that knows no North or South, no East or West, an America that is undivided by creed or color and untorn by suspicion or class. To those who have sought to divide us, they have only helped to unite us. To those who would provoke us, we have turned the other cheek. So, as we conclude our labors, let us tomorrow turn to our new task. Let us be on our way.

BRINKLEY: The Convention is adjourned and people are filing out. Now that the formal business of the Convention is all over, Chet, it seems to me that there are five or six names and faces that are and will be memorable from this week. The nominees themselves, of course. And Attorney General Kennedy tonight for his brief and eloquent tribute to his brother. Sen. McCarthy of Minnesota, who withdrew graciously from the contest, if there was a contest, for Vice President. Sen. Pastore and a rousing keynote speech. Mrs. John F. Kennedy, who flew here for a reception and shook several thousand hands, and with tears in her eyes said a few words about her late husband.

And then, of course, there was Judge Roy McCord, whom Frank McGee interviewed here the other night. He signed the loyalty oath but he refused to turn his back on his friends.

HUNTLEY: There might be another one you could add to that list, David. We didn't see too much of him to be sure, but nevertheless what he did was impressive. That was the Governor of Georgia—Gov. Sanders. Many of the great voices of the South of former years were not here. But this Governor of the State of Georgia is an impressive figure and he did play an important role in this Convention. And a final word about the great, perhaps unrecognized, development of this Convention. A small beginning has been made along a slow process of transforming the expression of the Negro's demands from sit-ins and picket lines to political action. Both whites and Negroes are going to make mistakes; there will be setbacks; but it will be a better day for everyone when the Negro's revolution can move out of the streets and out of the aisles and into the voting booths and the Convention.

BRINKLEY: We've received a wire saying that Chet and I have been sitting up here fat, dumb and happy while the men down on the floor have been kicked, punched, gouged, bitten, shoved, elbowed and stepped on. It's true. The floor correspondents have been doing the work, so we're going to get all of them together and have a relaxed kind of conversation with them about their week on the floor.

CHANCELLOR: Rational analysis may be difficult, but I think impressions stay in the mind about a Convention like this. The point I want to make is that I had quite an experience tonight, because on this Convention floor and in this giant arena, one man held the Convention in the palm of his hand for more than half an hour—his name was John Kennedy. The floor came alive when his brother, the Attorney General, Robert Kennedy, came up on the podium. I have in my mind been unable to make any determination of how much of this was for the Attorney General himself and how much of it was the expression of the outburst of sympathy and affection these people had been

138

waiting to give to John Kennedy. It was perhaps a mixture, but whatever it was, it was a moving moment on the floor.

VANOCUR: The Kennedy people know that President Kennedy is gone, and he won't come back. They know that their dominance in the Party is not going to be what it used to be under President Kennedy. They accepted this, but still you can't come to this place without being affected by the wave of nostalgia that passed over them when they saw Robert Kennedy, who is the repository of the faith they had in his brother.

The one thing that has satisfied the Northerners and Westerners, and made them feel that they still have a hold in the Party, is the selection of Hubert Humphrey — for in his own way, Humphrey has built up a great base in the large urban centers of the East and West. He is now going to try, I think, to form a bridge to the South, based on his strong support of agriculture. Many small farmers in the South are acquainted with Humphrey's record.

So, in this sense, there is a reconciliation here of the South with the North, and it was Lyndon Johnson, as head of the Party, who allowed the Southerners to make this reconciliation.

NEWMAN: I was interested not only in the reaction to President Kennedy, but in the reaction to President Johnson. I think the reaction of this Convention to the President was not emotional, but rather a feeling of gratitude.

They're grateful to him because he took up the torch after President Kennedy's death and he carried on, kept the Party going, kept the administration going, apparently very successfully. It doesn't make any difference which part of the country they're from, because he is not a sectional candidate. He apparently can be put forward pretty successfully with labor and the other big voting battalions in the big Northern cities.

Southerners and Westerners feel comfortable with Mr. Johnson. They think they understand him, and he thinks he understands them. And there is the element of respect for Mr. Johnson as a politician. We've seen a great example of it here at this Convention. There is nothing that Mr.

Johnson will not do to carry his Party into that campaign successfully. And I think there's a good deal of awe here, in the way he manages things.

Finally, Mr. Johnson is the man who has the responsibility of trying to keep the Democrats in office this fall, and that is sufficient to make any Democrat cheer him. When people at a Convention cheer, they cheer not only because they want the candidate to hear it, but because they want the rest of the country to hear it, too.

McGEE: I'd like to mention something that happened last night. If you will remember, we had three white members of the Regular Mississippi delegation who had signed the loyalty pledge and had taken their seats. And we had seven to nine Negro members of the Freedom Democratic Party who came and stood on the seats in front of these three. Those three white Mississippians sat there in their seats for perhaps an hour with their view of the podium and proceedings blocked. It was hot and it was stuffy, and there was a telephone there, and they could have been in communication with officials behind the scenes at any moment.

But they lodged no protest. They did not ask that the standees be removed. Had they made such a request, the sergeant at arms would have had no choice but to try to comply. But they did not protest; and because they did not, what could have been a nasty scene was avoided.

Now, there were only three of them. Most of the Mississippians went home, but those three who stayed last night were gentlemen, and they demonstrated something that needs to be demonstrated to us all from time to time: that everyone down there is not a red-neck, and they are not all fiercely militant on this subject, although they do hold their deep convictions. I, for one, felt that they were entitled to some tribute for this.

This Convention has done precisely what it was expected to do. It did, of course, nominate Lyndon Johnson for President of the United States. It did, of course, accept and nominate his recommendation for running mate. The platform was easily predictable if you looked back to what happened only a few weeks before in San Francisco.

But there was one thing that it had not expected to do that it did do, and I suspect that this might be rather like a time bomb that will come to our attention again in 1968, and that's the result of the fight before the Credentials Committee. It passed a proviso that at the next national Convention no delegate shall be seated if it can be established that segregation policies have been practiced in that State and in the selection of that delegate.

This can be the basis for challenge after challenge after challenge, but this is the real fruit of the work that was carried on here by the Freedom Democratic Party. I don't think that the Democrats really wanted to face up to the issue this time—I can't imagine any political party that really likes to face up to terribly difficult and controversial issues. But they had no alternative. Why did they not have an alternative? If I can order my thoughts here, I'd like to trace it back a little bit. When the Credentials Committee met, it was not expected that the Freedom Democratic Party would be able to muster enough strength there to get a minority report. But half of that committee is made up of women, and suddenly they had more than enough support to get a minority report. What was it that influenced the women on this committee? It was the testimony of a Negro woman from Mississippi, Fanny Lou Hamer. And they sat in that hearing room and heard her tell this tale about how she was taken one day to a jail in Mississippi, and how white officers ordered Negro prisoners to take blackjacks and beat her, how they sat on her legs and how they held her head down, and another indignity—when once her dress rose above her hips and she had the presence of mind to try to pull it down—a white officer pulled it up again and the beating continued. That moved them very deeply, and it provided the strength needed to get this compromise resolution. What I'm trying to say is that what happened in a stifling little jail in a sultry little town in the Mississippi Delta, set waves in motion that have already washed up on some distant shores. And I suspect that we'll hear more of this as time goes on.

CAPTIONS

THE CAMPAIGNS

THE PRELIMINARY ROUND

Although Presidential campaigns are traditionally launched in September, Sen. Goldwater actually begins his in July with his acceptance speech at the Republican Convention. After this speech, a number of prominent Republicans running for the Senate and House announce that their campaigns will be run separately from the national ticket. Among them are Gov. Romney in Michigan, and Sen. Keating and Rep. John Lindsay in New York. Others say they will await clarification of Sen. Goldwater's remarks on extremism.

On July 18, just two days after the Republican Convention, headlines throughout the nation report a riot that envelops Harlem, the Negro section of New York City. It is triggered by the killing of a Negro high school boy by a white policeman. For four nights the area is the scene of gunfire, fighting mobs, and looting. It becomes evident that the "white backlash" issue will figure prominently in the political campaign.

On July 20, in answer to a question from a newsman, Sen. Goldwater says he would be willing to meet with President Johnson to discuss the civil rights issue. There is talk that a way may be found to keep it out of the campaign. Asked about this at his news conference, the President agrees to meet with the Senator, but says: "I do not believe any issue which is before the people can be eliminated from the campaign in a free society in an election year...To the extent that Sen. Goldwater differs [with the Democrats on civil rights] there will, of course, be discussion. And I intend to carry on some of it if I am a candidate." On July 24, Sen. Goldwater goes to the White House, and the two meet for just 16 minutes. Afterwards, the White House issues a brief statement: "The President met with Sen. Goldwater and reviewed the steps he has taken to avoid the incitement of racial statements. Sen. Goldwater expressed his position, which was that racial tension should be avoided. Both agreed on this position." That very night, another riot breaks out, this time in the Negro district of Rochester, N. Y. It continues through July 26. There are other flare-ups through the summer, the next big one in Philadelphia on Aug. 28-30. Some Negro leaders, concerned about the "backlash" effect, urge a moratorium on all Negro demonstrations until after the election.

On Aug. 6, Sen. Goldwater meets with Gen. Eisenhower at Gettysburg and says afterward that Ike is "very enthusiastic" about the Republican ticket. On Aug. 7, Gov. Rockefeller says he will not campaign for Sen. Goldwater, but will concentrate on Sen. Keating's re-election instead. That same day, Sen. Goldwater writes a letter to Richard Nixon

clarifying his statements about extremism and moderation, and the Senator's explanation receives wide publicity. He says that in his acceptance speech he meant "that whole-hearted devotion to liberty is unassailable and that half-hearted devotion to justice is indefensible." Then, on Aug. 12, in an effort to solidify the Republican Party, Sen. Goldwater attends a unity conference in Hershey, Pa., with Gov. Scranton as host. Also attending are Gen. Eisenhower, Gov. Rockefeller, Gov. Romney, Rep. Miller, Mr. Nixon, and every Republican governor or candidate for governor. Here, Sen. Goldwater delivers a speech that was planned during his Aug. 6 visit with Gen. Eisenhower. Indeed, it develops that two former Eisenhower aides helped draft the address in which Sen. Goldwater charges that those who say his election would mean war are guilty of "the supreme political lie." At the Hershey meeting, the Senator promises to confer with Gen. Eisenhower and Mr. Nixon before picking his Secretaries of State and Defense, and says he would insist on "faithful execution" of the civil rights laws. Sen. Goldwater also insists that he favors stronger Social Security, that he is against extremists, and he singles out the Ku Klux Klan as an extremist group whose support he does not want. After the conference, Gen. Eisenhower says, "I am right on [Sen. Goldwater's] team as much as he wants me." Asked if he will campaign, Gen. Eisenhower says, "Well, I just remind you that I'll be 74 in October." Gov. Rockefeller says he feels better about things now, and will campaign for Sen. Goldwater, but not outside New York.

On Aug. 19, Sen. Goldwater appears at the Illinois State Fair and says, "There is a mood of easy morals and uneasy ethics that is an aching truth in our land." He decries "pitting class against class, race against race to reap votes."

On Sept. 2, the Senate passes by 49 to 44 a Social Security amendment providing medical care to the aged. This is a triumph for President Johnson, but Sen. Goldwater votes against it, saying: "Having given our pensioners medical care...why not food baskets...why not vacation resorts, why not a ration of cigarettes for those who smoke and beer for those who drink?"

THE FIRST WEEK

On Thursday, Sept. 3—speaking from the steps of the courthouse in the sun-splashed town square of Prescott, Arizona—Sen. Goldwater formally opens his campaign. Prescott is a good-luck town for the Senator. Here he delivered the kick-off speeches for his two successful Senate campaigns. Here his immigrant grandfather, "Big Mike" Goldwasser, settled after arriving from Poland. And here his uncle served as Mayor for almost a quarter of a century. Now, the Senator launches his campaign with a speech covering many of the issues he will stress during the nine weeks that lie ahead. He refers to civil rights: "Those who break the law are accorded more consideration than those who try to enforce it...Our wives, all women, feel unsafe on our streets." He talks of the nuclear issue: "I do not intend to be a wartime President." He makes coast-to-coast headlines by saying he will end the draft "as soon as possible—that I promise you!" And he issues a call for all voters to assemble under his banner: "I ask you to join with me in proving that every American can stand on his own, make up his own mind, chart his own future, keep and control his own family, asking for help and getting help only when truly overwhelming problems, beyond his control, beset him."

Two days later, Saturday, Sept. 5, both Vice Presidential candidates open their campaigns. Rep. William Miller, speaking in his home town of Lockport, N. Y., is joined by Sen. Goldwater. He assails Sen. Hubert Humphrey as a "radical." Rep. Miller flays the Americans for Democratic Action as an organization bent on changing the government into "a foreign socialistic totalitarianism." He links Sen. Humphrey with every position ever supported by the ADA, including recognition of Red China.

Rep. Miller's attack is so strong that Sen. William Fulbright (D., Ark.) rises on the Senate floor in Washington to accuse him of "foul-mouthed vituperation." Sen. Dirksen, the Republican Senate leader, comments only that Rep. Miller's attack was "a very earthy thing."

The same day, Sen. Humphrey opens his campaign back home in Minneapolis, where he declares that the principal issue of the campaign will be: "Which candidate is best equipped intellectually and emotionally to assume responsibility of leading this nation and the free world?"

Monday, September 7, is Labor Day. NBC News reports.

BRINKLEY: Since Harry Truman did it in 1948, all Democratic candidates for President have officially opened their campaign with speeches in Cadillac Square, Detroit. President Johnson did it today—but he said it wasn't official. It was a speech, however, and it was political. And the Democratic Party, not the government, paid for flying him there and back.

PRESIDENT JOHNSON: I am not the first President to speak here in Cadillac Square. I do not intend to be the last one....Make no mistake. There is no such thing as a conventional nuclear weapon. For

19 peril-filled years, no nation has loosed the atom against another. To do so now is a political decision of the highest order. It would lead us down an uncertain path of blows and counter-blows whose outcome none may know. No President of the United States can divest himself of the responsibility for such a decision....Those nations or individuals who seek to divide us, who preach strife and dissension and hate and fear and smear, strike at our hopes and the hopes of all the world.

PETTIT [in Detroit]: When President and Mrs. Johnson arrived at Cadillac Square, they received a tumultuous welcome from a crowd estimated at more than 100,000. In his speech, the President called for national unity, and he said the nation's goals are "prosperity, justice and peace." Opening with a peroration that wasn't part of the official text, he harked back to a day long ago, when he dreamed of a time when "the least among us will find contentment, and the best among us will find greatness, and all of us will respect the dignity of the one and admire the achievements of the other. ...This is what America is really all about." After the speech, and so much handshaking that his hand was bleeding, he flew back to Washington.

RON NESSEN [NBC Radio in Washington, D.C.]: Political observers think there may be a certain backlash in the nuclear issue, as there is in civil rights. For every voter who agrees with Goldwater, how many will be frightened over to Mr. Johnson's side by the mere mention in the campaign of setting off atomic bombs? In Detroit today, Mr. Johnson clearly meant to imply that he is restrained while Goldwater is trigger happy. He turned to the Bible for this passage: "He that is slow to anger is better than the mighty; he that ruleth his spirit is better than he that taketh a city." Two weeks ago, Goldwater set forth his nuclear position in a speech to the Veterans of Foreign Wars Convention.

GOLDWATER: I have suggested, along with many responsible leaders who consider the problem, that a way must be developed to provide NATO with its own stock of small, tactical, battlefield nuclear weapons, what may truly be called conventional weapons. And let me stress something

149

that the American people don't seem to understand—because they are not given the opportunity to understand: these small, conventional, nuclear, tactical weapons are no more powerful than the firepower you have faced on the battlefield. They simply come in a smaller package.

NESSEN: While President Johnson was calling for "national unity" in Detroit, Rep. Miller spent Labor Day in Indiana.

CHARLES QUINN [NBC Radio in South Bend]: William Miller's theme in Indiana has been the race issue. He doesn't call it that, but incessantly he pounds away at crime and violence in the streets. Miller also stressed that the man talking about the backlash or whitelash or any other kind of lash is not Barry Goldwater, but Lyndon Johnson.

In his Labor Day speech, Rep. Miller also accuses President Johnson of advocating that the United States "open the floodgates for virtually any and all who wish to come and find work in this country." Two days later Sen. Humphrey retorts: "When did Congressman Miller lose faith in America? We are a nation of immigrants... If present law were in effect one hundred years ago, Sen. Goldwater's grandfather possibly could not have come to the United States." The Democrats seize the issue and use it against the Republicans time and again when addressing ethnic groups. In the next four days, charges, promises and angry rebuttals are fired off with a rapidity that is unusual so early in a campaign.

In Washington, Sen. Fulbright says, "Goldwater Republicanism is the closest thing in American politics to an equivalent of Russian Stalinism. Each is convinced that there can be no peace in the world until its own ideology is universally practiced."

In Los Angeles, on Sept. 8, before more than 50,000 excited partisans who jam into Dodgers Stadium, Sen. Goldwater proposes a five per cent tax cut each year for five consecutive years. Sen. Humphrey, on Sept. 10, charges that Sen. Goldwater's tax cut proposal would "wreck the economy and set off an orgy of inflation." The same night, addressing a packed hall in Minneapolis, Sen. Goldwater says: "You know in your hearts something is wrong in your land... A lack of leadership has turned our streets into jungles, brought our public and private morals into the lowest state of our history, and turned out the lights even at the White House itself... The present administration has brought the Federal government snooping.

151

probing, grabbing, even strong-arming into more of your private life...." Next day, Robert MacNeil, traveling with the Goldwater campaign, reports from Chicago.

MacNEIL: Sen. Goldwater and his staff are elated with the results of their first intensive campaign week through Northern tier States. They claim their campaign has not only been launched, but has "taken off," and that their enthusiastic reception has been a better indication of public mood than the polls which show him running far behind President Johnson.

A newly aggressive Goldwater has emerged this week, in which his campaign jet has covered 8,000 miles. Where previously he shied away from crowds, he now plunges in, not yet with the abandon of Lyndon Johnson but, for Goldwater, something new. The Senator spent 45 minutes in a chaotic tour of a Polish museum in Northwest Chicago and talked about his Polish grandfather, Michael Goldwasser, who founded the Goldwater family in Arizona. He ate the traditional Polish symbols of "hospitality and wisdom," bread and salt, and waded through the rough and tumble of photographers and local politicians competing for his attention. After lunch he appeared before the annual conference of the American Political Science Association to argue that the Supreme Court was perverting its constitutional function:

GOLDWATER: I weigh my words carefully when I say that of all three branches of our government, today's Supreme Court is the least faithful to the constitutional tradition of limited government.

PETTIT [From Washington]: The White House has been President Johnson's best forum in the political campaign. His official actions as President got as much attention as Goldwater's political activities. For example, the President's sudden decision to leave the White House for an inspection tour of hurricane disaster areas emphasized his image of executive, rather than political action. But there is another part of the strategy. It was demonstrated last night at a Democratic dinner in Harrisburg. Mr. Johnson seemed to be courting what he calls the "frontlash" vote of Republicans who have doubts about Goldwater. He called on Pennsylvania Republicans to join him in a spirit of unity, and he claims that three out of ten Republicans will not vote for Goldwater. By aiming his remarks at them, Mr. Johnson is able to publicize his posture as the champion of unity, prosperity, peace and responsibility.

McGEE [Special report, Sept. 12]: Race will be to the Presidential campaign this year what religion was four years ago, despite the stated wishes of both candidates that it not be. It will be the paramount issue, but it will be submerged and imponderable. It is possible to campaign on race, wittingly or unwittingly, without appearing to do so, because certain words and phrases are taken to mean what they do not say specifically; not only new ones like "lawlessness in the streets," but older ones like "limited government" and "personal liberties." Regardless of the intent of the speaker, many listeners believe that such expressions are aimed at the Negro. A listener can, of course, either approve or disapprove.

In the South, many approve of the conservative philosophy of government as defined by Sen. Goldwater. They also approve of his vote against the civil rights bill. Taken together, they have given Goldwater a hold on the Old Confederacy that no Republican candidate before him has ever had, and he is banking on their electoral votes, which make up a quarter of the nation's total. With these, plus California, Texas, Illinois, Ohio, and the smaller Western States, Goldwater says he can win.

On Wednesday, Sept. 9, Governor Paul Johnson issued Mississippi's declaration of independence from the national Party.

GOV. JOHNSON: Mississippi's debt to the national Democratic Party is now paid in full...I am certain that our good conservative Mississippi voters will be talking and thinking about our constitutional government and their personal freedom, about the threats to local self government and individual liberty...When our good people vote their convictions on election day, I predict that the con-

153

servative American candidate will carry the State of Mississippi with a tremendous majority.

McGEE: Now, a series of reports from across the country, beginning with the Northeast.

MUELLER: The Northeast—thirteen States and Washington, D.C., from Maine to the Virginias —contains a quarter of the nation's population, and almost one-third of the Presidential vote. The region contains two-thirds of all the Negro districts outside the South, and half of the nation's worst unemployment pockets. It's no wonder that civil rights is the explosive number one issue, brought to the fore by the recent riots in New York, New Jersey and Pennsylvania.

The so-called backlash from threatened jobs, communities and schools is immeasurable. Yet, racial issues are further confused by the fact the Northeast contains 38 of the 50 largest ethnic or foreign population communities in the country. Their feelings often bypass bigotry to center on the second issue, nuclear policy or peace.

Concern about defense, concern about the value of the dollar and Social Security, and concern about local issues have led to restlessness in the area and numerous voter registration cross-overs. The Northeast expects a vituperative campaign.

KALBER: Here in the Midwest you hear talk about big government, government spending, South Vietnam, and foreign policy—but all of these are overshadowed by two main issues, the possibility of a civil rights backlash vote and discontent among the farmers.

The huge auto-making complex in Detroit, the steel centers of northern Indiana and South Chicago, the other highly industrialized cities of the Midwest are the backlash breeding grounds. There is civil rights resentment in all of these cities. But it's virtually impossible to measure that feeling.

Farm leaders point out that farmers are as concerned about government spending, foreign policy and civil rights as city folks, but there are some main farm problems. Probably the major issue is farm income. It has been dropping for several years and it will have its biggest drop this year.

157

ELMER PETERSON: Here in the West, Sen. Goldwater has completed his first week of full time campaigning. His emphasis on California showed again how determined the Republican nominee is to win California, both for its 40 electoral votes and its psychological importance to the future of the conservative movement. Defense spending, so vital to the West, will be one issue. Mr. Goldwater has been pointing to empty aircraft factories in the San Diego area. Water for the West will be a campaign issue, as will the argument over importing Mexican farm labor. Mr. Goldwater has indicated he will take the side of the California farmers who want Mexican labor. Civil rights promises to become a strong issue, and Goldwater supporters hope they'll be helped by the move to repeal California's fair housing act.

McGEE: Sen. Goldwater has taken the early offensive in the campaign. This is a necessity for him because he's trailing in the polls, and because he's facing the formidable task of dislodging the occupant of the White House. Last week [Sept. 3], at his hilltop home in the desert just outside Phoenix, Sen. Goldwater sat by the swimming pool and talked with Robert MacNeil:

MacNEIL: Senator, how is this campaign going to be different from other campaigns?

GOLDWATER: I think it will be different probably on the other side. I understand the President doesn't intend to do any active campaigning, or very little of it, relying on Humphrey. Bill Miller and I will work in concert across the United States. He'll be in one part, I'll be in another, and we're going to depend more and more on television and radio, as I think they will.

If you get down to the arithmetic of trying to see 182 million people in the next sixty days, you can't do it personally. More and more, I think campaigning depends upon good television and radio, plus press coverage. Actually, it's getting back to the older days where the candidate didn't campaign too actively. We went from that cycle to extreme activity like Dick Nixon tried to do—every State, working day and night and he wore

himself out. We don't think we can do that.

MacNEIL: Then, you plan a front porch or back patio campaign, with television?

GOLDWATER: To some extent. I will be traveling constantly by air and also by train. I have one swing through Ohio, Indiana and Illinois, about a four day trip by train—the old whistle-stop idea —but we still have this problem of getting to the people an image of what you are really like and what you really believe.

MacNEIL: What are the main issues you'll stress?

GOLDWATER: Foreign policy; our declining prestige around the world; our declining military strength; the moral situation here in the United States; the disregard of law and order, and the seeming disregard at the administrative level about lawlessness in this country.

MacNEIL: How are you going to counter the issue that the President will make much of, that the country is prosperous and peaceful?

GOLDWATER: The country is prosperous but it's not peaceful. We're in war in South Vietnam. I don't care what he wants to call it, but when you're killing American boys, you're losing American equipment, you're in war. Now, we'll admit that the economy is in good shape. We're not going to try to dispute that. But we will suggest that we haven't solved the problem of unemployment and we're not even working on it. We will suggest the future dangers—the dangers that are here today in the economy that will not come out until maybe a year from now unless we change some of the things we're doing. I happen to believe that a balanced budget, done carefully, could result in an annual income tax cut for several years in order to produce more capital investment. I don't think this last tax cut was wise because it was politically motivated. If we balance the budget and do it cautiously, carefully, I think we can have annual tax reductions with annual balanced budgets.

MacNEIL: What are you going to do about civil rights? Are you going to make speeches advocating enforcement of the bill that you voted against?

GOLDWATER: I've already made my position adequately clear on that, I believe. Any man elected

President is sworn to uphold the law and I've said that I would certainly do that, including all laws, which would include the recently passed civil rights bill. I think we ought to give this bill a chance. I think the less attention either side pays to it, the better chance it will have to work. If we say the wrong thing and incite passion on either side, then we're not giving a law passed by the majority of Congress a chance. Let's see a year from now or two years from now what it needs. It might need changing here or there, weakening or strengthening here or there, but we can't say now. I don't see how a candidate could intelligently discuss the civil rights law that was passed just two months ago.

McGEE: Sen. Goldwater, in person, belies the aggressive nature of his beliefs. Those who have read Goldwater in print—and much has appeared under his name—are often surprised when they see him or hear him for the first time. His mild, almost understated approach to a political interview or a speech is not expected by most. The exposure of a nationwide campaign should help correct those misimpressions. Now, an evaluation of the candidates, their strategy, and style so far.

MacNEIL: Sen. Goldwater now has a week's intensive campaigning under his belt and he seems very pleased with himself. His staff says he was seen by a quarter of a million people in the last ten days. Reporters, adding up their crowd estimates, make it about a hundred and fifty thousand. The crowds were exceedingly enthusiastic—"wild" is not too strong a term when the Senator was delivering set speeches from a text. They were somewhat more subdued but still aroused when he was making impromptu speeches. Goldwater appears to relish his role as a jet-age campaigner, swooping out of the skies in his Boeing 727 to small places where jets have never landed before, sleeping in one of the comfortable bunks, eating, working, playing with his ham radio rig, or occasionally taking the controls of the plane as it covers the country at almost 700 miles an hour. This fast, efficient, com-

fortable travel seems to have made Goldwater a less reluctant campaigner. He lingers after a speech to shake hands. In San Diego, astonished reporters even saw him kiss a baby, although he hasn't exactly made a habit of it.

He's pulled out so many stops so early in the campaign that one wonders how many he has left for the seven weeks ahead. He's called President Johnson power mad, accused the administration of manipulating foreign affairs for political ends, and of inciting violence by trying to legislate morality. His language gets tougher by the speech, his references to President Johnson more contemptuous. Goldwater often mentions spontaneously how badly he's doing in the polls. He says variously that he's always been a political underdog, that the polls have been wrong all year, and that he expects what he calls "a great boo-boo" on election day. But in quiet moments he says that he expects the polls to change soon, and that he'll be in trouble if they don't.

McGEE: Now an appraisal of the campaign of the Republican Vice Presidential nominee, William E. Miller, from NBC's Richard Hunt in New York.

HUNT: Congressman Miller started out with the kind of energy usually seen at the end of the campaign. He toured seven States in seven days, speaking five or six times a day in New York, Indiana and New England. From the start, it was clear that he's been given three jobs: to wake up the local Republican Parties and unite them for the campaign, to keep jabbing at the Democrats, and to defend Barry Goldwater.

Everywhere he goes, Miller plugs for the local Republican candidate, regardless of how they feel about Goldwater. In his opening speech at Lockport, N. Y., he even spoke up for Sen. Kenneth Keating, who was conspicuously somewhere else when Goldwater came in for the day. And in almost every major speech, Miller throws a punch at some Democrat, from the President on down. But he spends most of his time talking about two things that seem to worry the Republicans. Again

and again, he says Barry Goldwater hates war. Again and again, he says Barry Goldwater likes the Social Security system.

One thing the professionals are watching is who shows up and who doesn't when a national candidate comes to town. This week Miller hit ten States in four days in the Midwest and Southwest. He has been talking to small audiences, mostly Republican regulars. He has a rough, rousing style, loaded with slogans and catch words, and the Party faithful seem to like the kind of ammunition he is giving them. But when he spoke in Topeka, Kan., neither of the two Republican Senators, Frank Carlson and James Pearson, came to hear him. In Wisconsin, Miller spoke at Beloit. But the Republican candidate for Governor, former Lt. Gov. Warren Knowles, wasn't there. Some of the political writers in the Midwest think they're all keeping their distance from the Goldwater-Miller ticket. Miller is a professional and a team player. He's aware that these things are going on, but he doesn't complain and he keeps on running as hard as he can.

McGEE: Goldwater, Miller and Humphrey are devoting full time to the campaign. President Johnson cannot. He has another job, but this is hardly a political handicap. A report on his campaign from Tom Pettit in Washington.

PETTIT: President Johnson said today he thinks his basic campaign organization is in good shape, but even some organization field workers are wondering when the President will put himself into open political combat. Well, he is biding his time. No incumbent President has ever gone all out until after October 1. Besides, Lyndon Johnson enjoys all the advantages that the incumbent always has. Every official act enhances his basic campaign posture as a man of action and responsibility. So, for the time being, he will let Goldwater make all the purely political speeches. Mr. Johnson has any number of public opinion polls which show him well out in front in most places, so there is no compelling need to campaign hard right now.

But Mr. Johnson is not inactive. On Monday in

Detroit, he talked about nuclear responsibility. On Wednesday at a news conference, he said he is doing something about civil disturbances by getting full FBI reports. On Thursday, in Harrisburg, he attacked extremism as an alien doctrine. Today [Saturday, Sept. 12], at a walking news conference, he said there is no need to involve the Supreme Court in a political campaign. All these things are aimed at Goldwater without mentioning him by name.

McGEE: Now, an appraisal of the Democratic Vice Presidential nominee, Hubert Humphrey.

SCHERER [from Denver]: Earlier today [Saturday, Sept. 12], after Hubert Humphrey had conducted us on a felicitous tour of the Humphrey family drugstore in Huron, S. D., and mixed a prescription just to show that he could still do it, his plane flew on to Rapid City. There in the bright sun of the airport he spoke of his role in the campaign. Mr. Humphrey said President Johnson is not going to have a chance to get out on the political hustings all the time. "I'm doing some of it for him." This was another way of saying what is more and more evident, Hubert Humphrey is Lyndon Johnson's lightning rod in this campaign. He is out on the front line, the target for Mr. Goldwater and Mr. Miller, and he is firing back. Arriving in Denver, Sen. Humphrey put it this way: "I'd rather have a man who drives a little fast than a man who has one foot on the brake and the rest of the time his car in reverse."

As for his opposite number on the Republican ticket, Mr. Miller, Hubert Humphrey never mentions him at all. The main target is Barry Goldwater. Watching Hubert Humphrey campaign, the one thing that shines through is that he enjoys it. He is a zestful, a natural campaigner. He would rather shake hands or give a speech than eat.

The Governor of Minnesota has proclaimed Hubert Humphrey "the happy warrior of this generation." Delighted, Humphrey has christened his airplane "The Happy Warrior." The United States will see a lot of both happy warriors between now and November.

THE SECOND WEEK

en. Goldwater makes his first campaign foray into the South. On September 15, he travels to Winston-Salem, N. C., and, in a three-day swing through Dixie, the Senator is greeted by the largest and most enthusiastic crowds he has yet seen. He surprises many by. the things he says, and by what he leaves unsaid. In Knoxville, the heart of TVA territory, he tells the crowd that he stands on his anti-TVA position. And, in St. Petersburg, Fla., where tens of thousands of citizens receive Social Security checks, he never once mentions the subject. In Tampa, with its large Latin population, he ignores Cuba.

In Greenville, S. C., over 15,000 turn out for an emotional meeting between Sen. Goldwater and South Carolina's Sen. Strom Thurmond, who has quit the Democratic Party to become a Republican. Later, Sen. Goldwater concedes that Sen. Thurmond's support could have "dangers and disadvantages" as well as advantages for the Republicans, since Sen. Thurmond is a national symbol of white supremacy. In Raleigh, N. C., Sen. Goldwater says that a "re-orientation of the two major Parties is underway," with "hundreds, thousands, millions" of Democrats defecting to the Republican cause. NBC reports from the South.

MacNEIL: There have been almost no Negroes visible in the Southern crowds for Goldwater, either as members of the audience or as pickets. The Senator's references to civil rights have been oblique only, but his frequent demands for a resurgence of states rights and his attacks on the Supreme Court have been the most wildly applauded of all his statements. He's put less emphasis here on crime in the streets, the phrase that is supposed to evoke the civil rights backlash in the North. The main theme has been what the candidate sees as the evil and ever-encroaching power of Federal government and a growing trend of socialism, all personified in Lyndon Johnson, whom Goldwater pictures as power mad and but a few breaths removed from a dictator. The Southern crowds lap all this up.

n Sept. 18, in Charleston, W. Va.—the heart of Appalachia—Sen. Goldwater calls the war on poverty "a phony," created "to further selfish, political ambitions." Later that day, on his first nationwide

television appearance during the campaign, the Senator says, "a deliberate campaign has been and is being waged to create [a trigger-happy] image of me...I pledge to you that my Presidency will be dedicated to securing lasting peace and to preserving it. I simply do not wish to see our nation so weakened and so disarmed that we can be insulted, assaulted, and eventually attacked—and have but one awful choice: either surrender or nuclear holocaust... We can only keep the peace if we are strong."

President Johnson, meanwhile, embarks on a five-State "non-political" tour, and David Brinkley remarks: "Officially, President Johnson has not even begun to campaign. But whatever he has been doing, he did some more of it today." During this single week, the President travels more than 7,000 miles and delivers nine speeches. Tom Pettit reports on the President's activities in the West.

PETTIT: The President proclaimed an electric power treaty with Canada. But he also proclaimed nuclear responsibility a major issue in the campaign. He praised his own pursuit of peace, our own missile preparedness, and he warned of the nuclear destruction it could produce.

In a strongly-worded speech in Seattle he said: "On the President's prudence and wisdom alone can rest the decision which can alter or destroy the nation." Mr. Johnson today continued his emphasis on peace.

The climax of his trip came in Sacramento with the disclosure of two new American defense systems; one against possible use of military satellites, the other a radar system that can "see" around the curvature of the earth. For the first time his trip took on the atmosphere of a political campaign. The California Democratic organization turned out a huge crowd, estimated at over 50,000.

President Johnson still does not mention Barry Goldwater, except by implication. This trip was regarded as government business, not campaigning, but it is part of the political dialogue. Everywhere, the President has portrayed his administration as the guardian of peace and prosperity.

On Saturday, Sept. 19, Senators Goldwater and Humphrey address a huge crowd at the National Plowing Contest in Buffalo, N.D. Sen. Goldwater promises, if elected, to "stop this bureaucratic meddling in your private affairs." Later, Sen. Humphrey, addressing the same audience, says Barry Goldwater's election would be "the death sentence to agriculture." He quotes from Sen. Goldwater's book, THE CONSCIENCE OF A CONSERVATIVE, which urges "prompt and final termination of the farm subsidy program." This, says Sen. Humphrey, "would impoverish farm people, wipe out billions in land values, ruin business on rural America's main streets, and solve absolutely nothing."

BRINKLEY: The campaign is now about two weeks old and the country actually has heard very little it hasn't heard before. There has not been a new or very interesting idea from either Party and the excitement so far is not overwhelming. Of course, if either Party has a sensation to drop, it would be poor tactics to do it now, because there is still time to counteract it. If either side figures it's in trouble, it may begin looking around trying to find a bombshell.

McGEE: The latest Gallup Poll gives an indication of which is greater, frontlash or backlash. It shows 27 per cent of the Republicans across the country planning to vote for Johnson, while eight per cent of the Democrats plan to vote for Goldwater. So, as of now, frontlash is out front and the Democrats are benefiting.

THE THIRD WEEK

The new polls show Sen. Goldwater still far behind, but he is buoyed by large, friendly crowds as he campaigns in Oklahoma, Texas, Kansas, Iowa, Wisconsin, New Mexico and New York. Further, he gets a big lift from a nationwide television appearance in his behalf by Gen. Eisenhower, who dismisses the charge that the Senator is a warmonger as "actual tommyrot." President Johnson campaigns from Atlantic City to Texarkana; addresses two huge union meetings; embraces the President of Mexico in El Paso, and spends the weekend at his Texas ranch.

Sen. Goldwater, still trying to counteract the nuclear issue, tells a Dallas audience that "no man anywhere wants peace more than I do." In Boston, John F. Kennedy's home town, he attacks "lawlessness" in an address before more than 20,000 in Fenway Park. In Albany, N.Y., he is

greeted by Gov. Rockefeller, who still refrains from an outright endorsement.

Sen. Humphrey opens the Democratic week on Sunday, Sept. 20, with an appearance on NBC's MEET THE PRESS program. "The issue of nuclear power is possibly the central issue in this campaign," he says. "What you need is a President who is experienced, reliable; who temperamentally is steady and calm and not at all impetuous. There are no little old conventional nuclear weapons. These are deadly, destructive, powerful..."

On Monday, in a walk-around-the-White House press conference, President Johnson says that he has decided to campaign "in many, many States." His reasons: "We think the people want to hear from us." The next day thousands of members of the steel workers union do just that in Atlantic City's Convention Hall. In a speech that brings the audience to its feet, cheering, the President says: "We have faith in America and not fear of the future, because you are strong men of vision, not frightened crybabies, because you know it takes a man who loves his country to build a house instead of a raving, ranting demagogue who wants to tear down one."

BRINKLEY: When he's in front of a big crowd, the President is inclined to respond to the crowd and to shout and to gesture broadly so he can be seen and heard in the back row. But that kind of speaking style is not very good television, where the view is close-up. He is working on the problem, as other politicians have, and finding that it is difficult to talk simultaneously to a big crowd in the hall, and to a television audience usually consisting of two or three people in one small room.

THE FOURTH WEEK

Although the polls point to overwhelming popular support for the President, he acts as if he were far behind. At eight o'clock Monday morning, Sept. 28, he goes on a whirlwind New England tour, and at four o'clock the next morning—20 hours later—the President is still at it. Enormous crowds engulf his motorcade—200,000 in Hartford, Conn. (the largest turnout ever, say the police); 70,000 in Portland, Me., (pop. 80,000). John Chancellor calls it "the most emotional and tumultuous reception" the President has experienced since taking office. Time after time he orders the motorcade to halt so he can talk to the crowds through his hand-held electric bull-horn. Time

after time, to the despair of his security officials, the President shouts at the struggling police to let the crowds through. The President is said to have been annoyed by those who contend that the people feel no warmth for him, so these 20 hours of roaring approval provide much satisfaction to him and his staff. In Burlington, Vt., he tells the crowd: "One of our great Parties has been captured by a faction of men who...have not just marched out of step with American progress; they have refused to march at all."

While the President is plunging through New England by car and jet, Sen. Goldwater is on a train, whistle-stopping through Ohio, Indiana and Illinois, three big States he says he must have for victory. In small and middle-sized towns and cities of this Republican heartland —often where no campaign train has stopped for a decade or more—he draws enthusiastic crowds. He leaves the train in Cincinnati for a major speech before 16,000 cheering supporters. There, Sen. Goldwater uses a phrase that brings back memories of an earlier era, and it stirs up a national storm: "I charge that this administration is soft on communism." Questioned by newsmen the next day, the Senator says Herbert Hoover and Richard Nixon suggested that he use the phrase. But Mr. Nixon, commenting in Boston, denies it. "I made no suggestion," he says. "There is no question of President Johnson's loyalty or anti-communism." And at a subsequent press conference, the President says, "This sort of nonsense is the product of some third-string speech writer. [Sen. Goldwater] is merely trying out this charge to see if it works. My own advice would be to drop it." Sen. Humphrey calls it "the last dying gasp of a desperate politician." But Sen. Goldwater uses it again during his whistle-stop speeches in Indiana and Illinois. In Des Moines, on Sept. 30, Sen. Humphrey says, "How strange to hear a pied piper of discontent traveling about America, teaching distrust and disunity, seeking to drive a wedge of suspicion between the government and the people." That same day, Ron Nessen reports from the Goldwater train.

NESSEN: All day long the candidate has carried on a kind of buck-shot campaign, attacking President Johnson and pushing his own ideas on a long list of issues, sometimes switching abruptly from issue to issue. Sen. Goldwater criticized the way foreign aid money is spent, called for the liberation from communism of Poland and Hungary, and charged President Johnson is claiming credit for the A-11 airplane when President Eisenhower really initiated it.

G en. Eisenhower, speaking at the New York World's Fair on Oct. 2, says, "The campaign is getting to be a confused state of affairs. I can't define the issues. I don't know—something's wrong."

While the General is at the World's Fair, his former Vice President, Richard Nixon, opens a campaign in which he will make 150 appearances in behalf of Sen. Goldwater. In Des Moines, conceding that the Senator has switched positions on a number of important issues, Mr. Nixon defends the action by saying: "A change of position by Mr. Goldwater is an action of principle. A change of views by President Johnson is an act of political expediency." On various other occasions during his tour, Mr. Nixon also makes the following comments about the Democratic candidates.

NIXON: I want to tell you about Hubert [Humphrey]. I want to be absolutely objective. There's no question—and I want you all to bear this in mind —Hubert's a loyal American. Hubert is against the communists. Hubert is for peace. Hubert's a very plausible man. He's a very pleasant man. He's a good campaigner. But Hubert is a sincere, dedicated radical...

NIXON [later]: I do not impugn the character of President Johnson, but I do say this: There is at present hanging over the White House a cloud. That cloud is there because President Johnson has refused to repudiate payoffs, influence peddling by his closest political associate, Bobby Baker. As a matter of fact, I was in Texas and the Texans say this Johnson administration is government of the birds, by the birds and for the birds.

THE FIFTH WEEK

N ow, the candidates pull out all the stops. Not only are all four stumping the country (53 cities in a single week), but even their wives are campaigning—Mrs. Peggy Goldwater in Indiana and Ohio, and Mrs. Johnson on a whistle-stop tour of the South. The President is acclaimed by more than 150,000 in Des Moines, Iowa, a State that has not gone Democratic since 1948. And he pulls tremendous crowds in Springfield and Peoria, Illinois.

On Monday, Oct. 5, Sen. Goldwater says: "If elected President, I will ask former President Eisenhower...to go

to South Vietnam and report back to me..." Asked about this statement, Gen. Eisenhower refuses to comment.

On Tuesday, Oct. 6, in a fashionable suburb of Philadelphia, Sen. Goldwater says the United States is run by "minority groups...who are able to put together an expensive lobby in Washington to make themselves heard." The Senator continues, "the forgotten American is the man who pays his taxes, obeys the law, but has no lobbyist."

That same Tuesday morning, Lady Bird Johnson sets off on her 1,800-mile whistle-stop train tour of the South. Nancy Dickerson, who accompanies the First Lady every mile of the way, reports.

NANCY DICKERSON: Mrs. Johnson's whistle stop was historic because this was the first time that a First Lady attempted one alone, and historic because it put petticoat politics in the Big League. It all started on a crisp fall morning in Washington. The President, the First Lady and their older daughter, Linda, boarded the train at Union Station. The President believed that if the South, traditionally Democratic but leaning toward the Republicans, was to be saved for his Party it was his wife who could do the most. After kissing her goodbye, the "Ladybird Special" was off.

A whistle stop is many things. It's the elective process in motion. It's also a traveling circus with all the hoopla and fanfare. The crowd, which often waited a long time, could hear the strains of "Hello, Lyndon" blaring from the loudspeakers on the train, and then the excitement would mount and everyone would be yelling as the train rolled to a stop. The "Ladies for Lyndon," dressed in red, white and blue, would get out and give souvenirs to the crowd—engineer hats, LBJ hats, and even salt water taffy. A speech and then a final wave from either Linda Johnson, who was there the first two days, or the younger Johnson daughter, Luci, who was there the last two.

As the North disappeared into the past, Mrs. Johnson was introduced in one place as the "First Lady of Dixie." In others she was hailed as a Southerner, and she always found there was something special about the South:

MRS. JOHNSON [speaking from rear platform of train]: I've heard it said, and I agree, that the South is not a matter of geography, but a place for the heart. And Georgia is not only a State. It is a distinctive part of America. America grows up smacking its lips over Georgia broiler chicken and Georgia peanut butter, drinking Coca-Cola, and I certainly don't want to leave out Talmadge ham. I have a lot of memories, that I know you share, of the South I knew in my childhood. I am fond of the old Southern custom of keeping up with your kinfolk, all your uncles and your aunts and your cousins; of long Sunday dinners after church, and of a summertime filled with watermelon cuttin's, swimmin' in the creek and visiting for weeks. I hope that South never disappears. My main reason for coming here today was to say to you that to this Democratic candidate for President and his wife, the South is a respected and valued and beloved part of this country.

NANCY DICKERSON: Generally the South loves Mrs. Johnson, hailing her as one of its own. But many Southerners also love Sen. Goldwater, believing him to be the candidate who best reflects their own traditionally conservative viewpoint. At every stop there were Goldwater signs. At first it was just signs, but in Columbia, S. C., there were chants of "We Want Goldwater!", and they were so loud it was impossible for Mrs. Johnson to continue with her speech.

MRS. JOHNSON: My friends, this is a country of many viewpoints, and I respect your right to express your own. Now it's my turn to express mine.

NANCY DICKERSON: The success of the whistle stop is measured by the size of the crowd, and they were far beyond expectation at every stop. Rep. Hale Boggs of Louisiana, who rode the whole way and spoke all along the way, won great shouts of approval from the crowds when he said: "Don't let anybody tell you that Lyndon Johnson isn't going to carry the South. He and his wife are as much a part of the South as tobacco and cotton and peanuts and grits and red-eye gravy and you name it, we got it!"

Mrs. Johnson's staff was frankly elated with the success of the trip, and they were cheering the loudest when the final whistle blew and a tu-

184

multuous welcome greeted the "Lady Bird Special" when it reached New Orleans.

MRS. JOHNSON [in New Orleans]: Unforgettable days. Eight States, 1,800 miles, about 48 speeches—and I have found that my Southland is moving forward with the times. It's been a journey of the heart, one that I will always love, one that I will always remember, because it proved to me that my South is going forward toward greener days, a day of peace among us all. Thank you for coming out, and God Bless You!

MacNEIL: On Oct. 7, Lyndon Johnson, formally and unashamedly became a candidate running for office. Starting a week-long tour of ten States, he issued a statement saying he was leaving to report to the people on his stewardship. Arriving at Des Moines for the first stop, the President hungrily waded into the crowds, and drew from them squeals of delighted, almost hysterical affection. So far, Sen. Goldwater has not yet found crowds that greet his in-the-flesh appearance with emotional displays of this kind. The crowd was so dense that several people fainted.

Next day, in East Chicago, part of the world's biggest concentration of heavy industry, there were very large crowds at the airport and along the route into town. Riding in his remodelled Lincoln Continental—the car in which President Kennedy was killed—he took to the roof. An anxious Secret Service man held his feet. Parts of this area—Lake County, which Gov. Wallace won in the Indiana primary—have Negro populations as high as fifty per cent. Large numbers of Negroes turned out for the President today and he took pains in his rapid progress through the crowds to pay attention to them. A band of Negro high school students caught his attention. He chatted for several minutes and told the students: "The whole country's watching you'all, and counting on you to make good...and I believe in you." Another vast crowd awaited him in Indianapolis. The President climbed to the photographers' platform and then, unable to find more of himself to give, threw them his grey felt ten gallon hat. Plastic LBJ hats were

handed up and he delightedly threw them to the squealing crowd. He looked as if he enjoyed this enough to go on doing it all day. As he came down, the President hunched his shoulders like a hungry man sitting down to a meal. Again he waded in as if no crowd could ever supply him with enough hands and voters to touch.

During the week, Sen. Goldwater was also speaking out vigorously. He charged that "we are headed for another war if we continue the silly notion that we have to disarm regardless of what our enemies do." And he said, "I wish the opposition Party would accept the term Socialist Party because . . . like it or not, this is the road they are on."

On Friday, Oct. 9, the President is in New Orleans to greet his wife at the conclusion of her whistle-stop train tour. And, in that city, before a huge Southern crowd, Mr. Johnson makes an impassioned speech in favor of civil rights.

PRESIDENT JOHNSON: I want us to put behind us the problems of the past, and turn toward the promise of the future here in the South and all across the land...

Posterity must know no Mason-Dixon line, and opportunity must know no color line.

THE SIXTH AND SEVENTH WEEKS

On Tuesday, October 13, Robert MacNeil reports from Washington: "When President Johnson crawled into bed in the White House shortly before dawn this morning, after a week's exposure to hundreds of thousands of people in fifteen States, he was a weary and happy man."

Many days are to pass before the President is that happy again. For, there occurs on Wednesday, Oct. 14, the first of a succession of major events that will affect not only the campaign but the rest of the world, as well.

Wednesday. It is revealed that Walter W. Jenkins, Special Assistant to the President, and Mr. Johnson's confidant for 25 years, had been arrested in a Washington YMCA on Oct. 7, for what police describe as "disorderly (indecent) gestures." And it is discovered that Mr. Jenkins had been arrested in 1959, in the same place, for "disorderly conduct (pervert)."

Thursday. Russia electrifies the world by ousting Pre-

mier Nikita Khrushchev from his government and Party posts, and by denouncing him for his "harebrained schemes." In England, the Labor Party wins the narrowest of election victories over the ruling Conservatives, and Harold Wilson becomes the new British Prime Minister.

Friday. Peking radio announces that the Chinese Communists have "exploded an atom bomb...and thereby conducted successfully its first nuclear test."

President Johnson is in New York City Wednesday when he gets the news about Mr. Jenkins. It is a shaken President who appears that night before the Alfred E. Smith Memorial Dinner, sponsored by Francis Cardinal Spellman, and he skips over large portions of the prepared text of his foreign policy address. The President's press secretary, George Reedy, tells a hurriedly called press conference that Mr. Jenkins has resigned and has entered a Washington hospital for "nervous exhaustion." Next day, the President issues a statement saying that "until yesterday, no information or report of any kind to me had ever raised a question with respect to [Mr. Jenkins'] personal conduct." Mr. Johnson orders a full and immediate investigation by the FBI.

Sen. Goldwater declares, "I do not intend to comment [on the Jenkins matter] at all." But he says he will speak out if issues of national security are involved. During the rest of the week, the Senator refrains from mentioning Mr. Jenkins by name, but he draws cheers and laughter whenever he refers to the President's "curious crew."

Mrs. Johnson, in a formal statement, says, "My heart is aching for someone who has reached the end point of exhaustion in dedicated service to his country." President Johnson, in another statement, says, "Walter Jenkins has worked with me faithfully for 25 years...No man I know has given more personal dedication, devotion and tireless labor..." The President says he asked for Mr. Jenkins' resignation because "the public interest comes before all personal feelings."

In Chicago, Rep. Miller asserts, "If this type of man had information vital to our survival, it could be compromised very quickly and very dangerously." Richard Nixon, referring to Mr. Jenkins and Bobby Baker, says the President's "two closest associates" were "bad apples." And Clifton White, director of Citizens for Goldwater-Miller, announces the formation of "Mothers For A Moral America," which will prepare a television film about what the Republicans term "immorality" in America.

MacNEIL: It was a subdued President Johnson who spoke in New York, with the most important statement of his foreign policy that the campaign has yet produced. This is part of what he said.

PRESIDENT JOHNSON: Because we have been responsible in control of our power, we have won the confidence of all who know the terrors of the atom...Almost all general statements about the world are wrong. They are not necessarily false. They are just inadequate. It is true that communism is a danger. But Russia is a different kind of danger from Yugoslavia. A small Communist Party in Africa is a different danger from the government of Red China. These different dangers require different policies, different actions and different replies. Beware of those who come to you with simple slogans. We will not permit the great civilizations of the East—almost half the people in the world—to be swallowed up in communist conquest. Let no one be foolhardy enough to doubt the strength of that unyielding American commitment.

MacNEIL [Oct. 15]: President Johnson went on campaigning today as though nothing had happened. He did not mention the Jenkins affair in public or in private. It appeared he had decided the best thing was to forget it and get on with the business of selling his program of what he calls responsibility abroad and compassion at home.

SCHERER [Omaha, Oct. 16]: Barry Goldwater made a marvelous nautical entrance today into Sioux City, Iowa. He came up the Missouri River in a tug named "The S. S. Goldwater." As the Senator came into the city, teenagers tossed an egg at him. It struck above his left ear and splattered on his sleeve. He said, "One of LBJ's boys hit me with an egg, but at least it's fresh." Then he went inside to speak on the farm program.

GOLDWATER: I pledge, as I have pledged before, that I will never propose a change in the price support program until something better has been developed that can gradually be substituted for it.

I will never jerk the rug from under the American farmer.

ABEL [Washington, Oct. 16]: President Johnson had planned to make two campaign speeches to-

night, in Cincinnati and Dayton, Ohio, and then spend the weekend on his ranch in Texas. He's decided now that he will instead spend the weekend in Washington, because of the numerous, rapid and important national and international developments.

GOLDWATER [Youngstown, Ohio, Oct. 17]: I am not overly impressed with [the Chinese bomb] because I have been convinced for a long time that almost anybody can make an atomic device if you get a little piece of fissionable material. I don't think you can make them in your kitchen, and you can't get do-it-yourself kits, but the fact that China has exploded a device doesn't mean that tomorrow she will become a nuclear threat."

*O*n Sunday night, Oct. 18—with the impact of the new governments in Russia and England, and the news of the Chinese explosion still reverberating around the globe—President Johnson appears before the people in a nationally televised address to reassure Americans, and to make the nation's position known to the rest of the world.

PRESIDENT JOHNSON: [Khrushchev's government] had shown itself aware of the need for sanity in the nuclear age...[His successors] are experienced but younger men, perhaps less rooted in the past...We can hope that they will share with us our great objective—the prevention of nuclear war...We must never forget that the men in the Kremlin remain dedicated, dangerous communists. A time of trouble among communists requires steady vigilance among free men, and most of all among Americans, for it is the strength of the United States that holds the balance firm against danger...[I have spoken] frankly, as always, to the Soviet Ambassador...I believe that this was a good beginning on both sides... [China's] nuclear pretensions are both expensive and cruel to its people...Nations that do not seek nuclear weapons can be sure that if they need our strong support against some threat of nuclear blackmail, then they will have it...Today [England's new Labor government] has the confidence of the British people. It also has ours...The

friendship of our two nations goes on...This has been an eventful week in the affairs of the world. It has not been the first such week, nor will it be the last...The world has changed many times in the last 20 years...Danger has taken the place of danger...The key to peace is to be found in the strength and the good sense of the United States of America...Tonight, as always, America's purpose is peace for all men.

The Republicans immediately demand equal television time, asserting that the President's speech is "political," but the Federal Communications Commission rejects the appeal, finding that the speech was a "bona fide news event," and the courts sustain the Commission. William R. McAndrew, Executive Vice President in charge of NBC News, wires Dean Burch that NBC agrees with the FCC's decision, but "in a spirit of fairness, we are prepared to give time for discussion of the Republican viewpoint on the international developments referred to by the President...We will make available to you personally, as Chairman of the Republican National Committee, an approximate 15-minute period Monday night, Oct. 19." Mr. Burch accepts, and during his appearance on NBC-TV he appeals for campaign funds. GOP officials subsequently report receiving 82,000 letters and 3,700 telegrams with contributions, more than had been received "throughout the entire 1960 Republican Presidential campaign."

Many Republicans assault the President's speech. Richard Nixon calls it "shocking," and asserts that it was designed to "lull the American people into thinking there was really no significant change" in the international situation. On Tuesday, Oct. 20, Sen. Goldwater attacks the Administration for its "Soft Deal for Communism." Rep. Miller claims "the ADA, the Liberal Party, and Socialist Party have taken over the Democratic Party lock, stock and barrel." In Long Island, N. Y., Mrs. Goldwater asks voters to cast their ballots for her husband. "I think you know him," she says. "His name is Barry."

Democratic National Chairman John Bailey attacks a Republican film, "Choice," sponsored by "Mothers For A Moral America," which is scheduled to be shown as a paid political broadcast on NBC-TV, Thursday, Oct. 22. The film includes scenes of a girl in a topless bathing suit, pornographic magazines, Negro riots, and a speeding limousine leaving behind a trail of empty beer cans — a scene purporting to reflect on President Johnson. Chairman Bailey calls the film "the sickest political program to be conceived since television became a factor in American

politics." But Russell Walton, public relations director for Citizens for Goldwater-Miller, says the film's purpose is "to portray and remind the people of something they already know exists, and this is the moral crisis in America, the rising crime rate, rising juvenile delinquency, narcotics, pornography, filthy magazines...We want to make their stomachs turn." On Wednesday evening, Oct. 21, David Brinkley reports.

BRINKLEY: The Republican documentary film showing what was said to be a growing immorality in the United States has been withdrawn. Dean Burch said this afternoon that Sen. Goldwater had asked that it not be shown. [The Senator subsequently called it "nothing but a racist film."] It was to have been put on NBC Television tomorrow as a paid political program. NBC looked at it and agreed to broadcast it if a few brief scenes were removed. The Citizens for Goldwater-Miller, which made the film, agreed to these few cuts. Apparently there are some differences of opinion within the Party. The National Committee objected to the film, but the Citizens for Goldwater-Miller wanted to go ahead with it. Morality, or immorality, now has become the dominant and most discussed issue in the Republican campaign.

That same day, Oct. 21, Sen. Goldwater formally replies to President Johnson's Sunday night television speech. He says the Democrats' foreign policy, "based on the belief that there are 'good' and 'bad' communists," has been "an utter failure." He says America must "recognize that communism is our enemy...and confront communism with a firm policy of resistance."

The FBI, which has been investigating the Jenkins affair, releases its report on Oct. 22. It concludes that there is no evidence that President Johnson had any knowledge of Mr. Jenkins' arrest record, and that there is no evidence that Mr. Jenkins "compromised the security...of the United States in any manner."

THE FINAL WEEK

Every poll indicates a smashing victory for President Johnson, but he and Senator Goldwater act as if the polls are wrong. The President dashes through the South, Midwest, and West Coast, shaking every hand in sight, imploring the voters to be sure to get to the polls, "and tell your uncles and your cousins and your aunts."

Sen. Goldwater begins his week on Monday night with

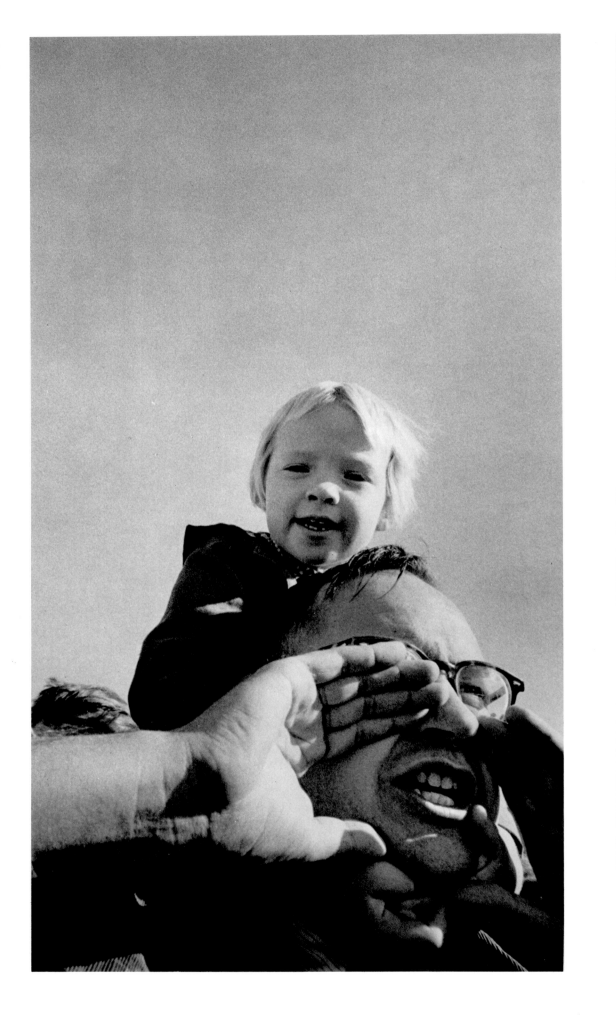

his only appearance of the entire campaign in New York City. Madison Square Garden is packed to the rafters with 18,000 ardent supporters, and more than 5,000 fill the streets outside. When the Senator enters the Garden, he is greeted by an explosion of cheers, whistles, gongs, drums, horns and screams. For 28 minutes the greeting shakes the Garden, and when the Senator is finally able to begin speaking, he is interrupted by cheers at virtually every sentence.

GOLDWATER: I want to tell you folks here in New York and all across the country that a week from tomorrow there will occur the major political upset of this century...If you ever hear me quoted as favoring the right to associate—without favoring the equally vital right not to associate—look again, because somebody will be kidding you...If you ever hear me quoted as promising to make you free by forcibly busing your children...just to meet an arbitrary racial quota—look again, because somebody is kidding you!

It is a fact that Lyndon Johnson and his curious crew seem to believe that progress in this country is best served simply and directly through the ever expanding gift power of the everlastingly growing Federal government. One thing we all know—and I assure you I do: that's a much easier way to get votes than my way. It's always been It's political Daddyism, and it's as old as demagogues and despotism...

I speak of peace. Your interim President tells you I want to start a war—which is ridiculous, and you know it, and he knows it. I speak of strengthening the Social Security system, and your interim President tells you I want to destroy it—which is ridiculous, and he knows it, and you know it. I refer to the fundamental principles on which our great country was founded, and my opposition tells you I am living in the past—which is ridiculous, and you know it, and he knows it...

Our government is in a state of moratorium until "after the election." And the office of President is being occupied, on a part-time basis, by the interim President, who's busy sweeping the business of his office under the rug with Bobby Baker, Billie Sol Estes, Matt McCloskey, and goodness

198

knows what else until after the election...

President Johnson, concentrating on States where he feels he is weakest, is in Columbia, S.C., saying that Sen. Goldwater has offered "the most radical proposals ever made to the American people." In Jacksonville, Fla., he talks about the candidates from Wilson to Nixon and Kennedy, and says that "none of these men tried to split our country wide open, none of these men preached hate."

On Tuesday, Sen. Goldwater speaks on civil rights to 14,000 supporters in Cleveland: "No person, whether government official or private citizen, should violate the rights of some in order to further the rights of others....We are being asked to destroy the rights of some under the false banner of promoting the civil rights of others."

MacNEIL: Like a medieval king rousing his forces before the battle, Sen. Goldwater flew into various of his strongholds today, preaching hope and breathing defiance of Lyndon Johnson. As his attack on the President sharpens, it is the image of the absolute monarch that he tries to invoke. In the deeply Republican parts of Tennessee and Kentucky, he blasted the President as a power-hungry man with a king complex. The big turn-outs of the last few days encourage the Senator—or his speechwriters—to claim that he, not President Johnson, has the real grass roots support. He continues to predict an upset, but privately even some of his own staff are saying "the polls can't be that wrong."

President Johnson talks to a large crowd in Pittsburgh, and mentions Mr. Jenkins for the first time before a campaign audience. He says that in government, men sometimes "disappoint you." In Boston, 350,000 people turn out for the President, who delivers a moving tribute to President Kennedy.

McGEE [Special report, Oct. 27]: Most Americans believe a Presidential campaign should be waged on the highest level, but only sometimes are their hopes realized. One organization trying to keep this campaign within some bounds of decency is the Fair Campaign Practices Committee, whose Executive Director is Bruce Felknor.

FELKNOR: This is a vicious campaign. I don't re-

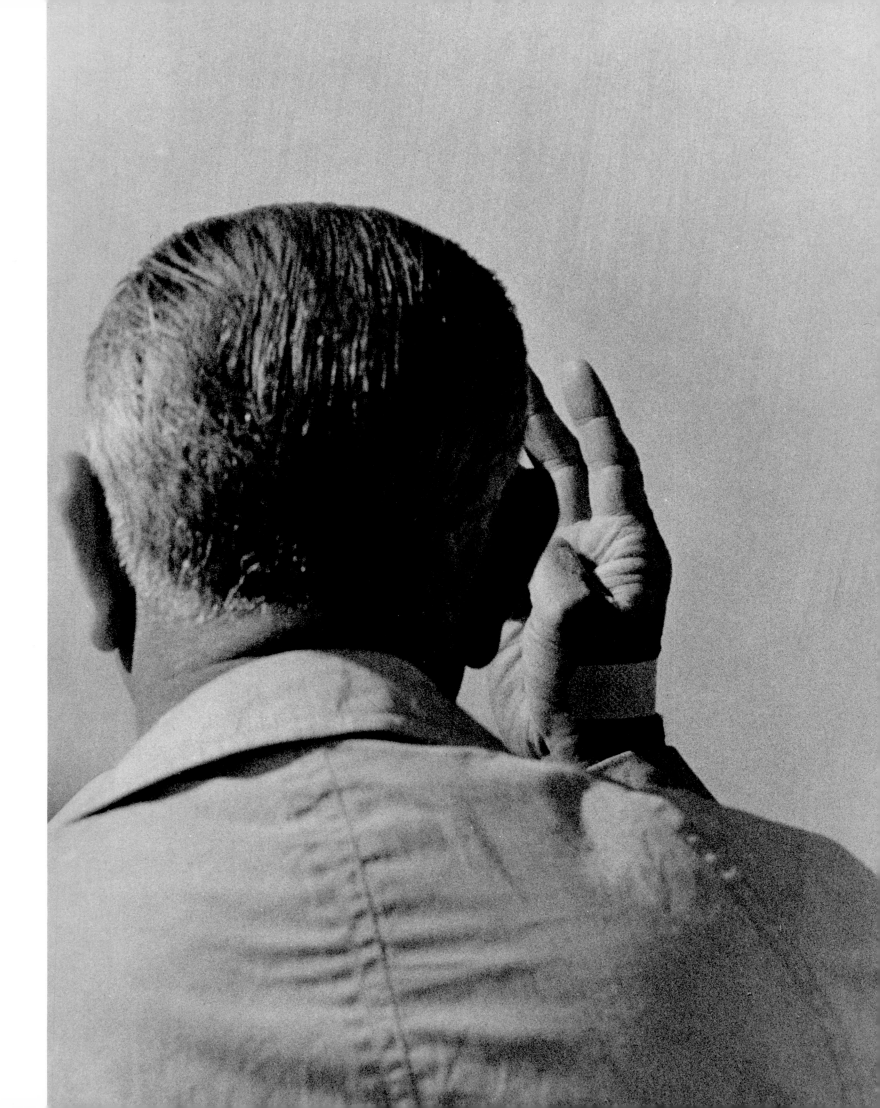

member anything like it. We've had serious suggestions that one candidate or the other is a maniac or a thief. Look back at the very start of the campaign to the Democratic TV spots of a little girl picking petals off a flower and boom, there's an atomic explosion—the implication that Goldwater is the man who's going to push the button, and watch out. No Party has a monopoly on virtue or stupidity. Look at the Republican movie suggesting that the Democratic Party is the patron saint of vice, immorality and everything else. Each is saying it about the other. It contributes to cynicism and disgust and confusion on the part of the voters. It certainly doesn't contribute to understanding the issues.

GOLDWATER [Cedar Rapids, Iowa, Oct. 28]: How can [churches] be concentrating on morality when we find clerical spokesmen who now become loud advocates of Lyndon Johnson?

PRESIDENT JOHNSON [Los Angeles, Oct. 28]: Some people have more guts than brains... Any jackass can kick down a barn, but it takes a carpenter to build one.

SCRANTON [Introducing Sen. Goldwater in Pittsburgh]: I do not believe in walking out on a Party.

PRESIDENT JOHNSON [Rockford, Ill., Oct. 30]: I have always been the kind of Democrat who could and would work together with [members] of the Party of Lincoln and McKinley, Herbert Hoover and Dwight Eisenhower, Robert Taft and Everett Dirksen... Good Republicans will consider seriously and soberly what is best for America, and will vote on no other basis."

O
n Saturday, Oct. 31, Sen. Goldwater is greeted by 50,000 people in Columbia, S.C. There he delivers a civil rights speech on a live television hookup of 14 Southern States. The Senator reiterates his civil rights theme: "We are being asked to destroy the rights of some under the false banner of promoting the civil rights of others."

That night, President Johnson appears in Madison Square Garden. As it was for Sen. Goldwater earlier in the week, the Garden is filled to its 18,000 capacity, and thousands stand in the streets outside. The President says of the Goldwater adherents' beliefs: "This is not a conservative philosophy. This is not even a Republican philosophy. 'Conservative' may be written on their banners and in their books, but 'radical' is in their hearts." America, the President continues, "has greatness almost within its grasp. This is the goal within our sight. This is the goal to which I pledge I will try to lead all of you."

On Sunday, Nov. 1, Dean Burch predicts that Sen. Goldwater will carry 28 or 29 States and will win the election. Kenneth O'Donnell, Executive Director of the Democratic National Committee, says President Johnson will carry every State except Mississippi and Alabama.

Monday night, November 2, 1964—election eve.

RUSS WARD [NBC Radio]: Fifty-six-year-old Lyndon Johnson is in his home State of Texas tonight, where he will await tomorrow's decision. Fifty-five-year-old Barry Goldwater will keep the watch at his home just outside of Phoenix. It has been a long campaign.

NESSEN [NBC Radio]: The public opinion polls, which say President Johnson will win by a landslide, also show that the main reason why voters apparently have rejected Goldwater is a fear that he would get the nation into a war. The same poll shows that 64 per cent think he would go to war with Cuba and almost 60 per cent think he would use atomic weapons in Asia. The only time political observers hesitated in their prediction that Mr. Johnson would win big was when the Walter Jenkins case broke. But the day after the revelation, Nikita Khrushchev was ousted as Russian Premier and the day after that Red China exploded its first atomic bomb. These developments stole the headlines from the Jenkins affair. The Jenkins case might have helped Sen. Goldwater's cause, except for the big foreign developments which historically have tended to help the President already in office.

ABERNETHY [NBC Radio]: Just a few days ago, Sen. Goldwater rode a train through the bleak old Pennsylvania towns between Harrisburg and Pittsburgh, speaking at each stop on one central

theme: his position on Social Security. This was typical of Senator Goldwater's major problem. He can never really get off the defensive. Since his battles with Nelson Rockefeller in the primaries and with William Scranton just before the Republican Convention, Mr. Goldwater has borne brands that neither oratory nor travel have been able to hide. Sen. Goldwater has laid out his issues with great sincerity. He insists there is too much power in the hands of the President, that immorality in Washington affects the whole society, that the administration has been soft on communism, and that in race relations, the right not to associate is just as precious as the right to associate. Sen. Goldwater insists that what's called a silent vote will bring about the century's major political upset. But it may be that by tomorrow night the silent vote will appear to have been in the same category as those things from which the Scots once asked deliverance, "ghoulies and ghosties and things that go bump in the night."

BRINKLEY: Finally—now that the campaign is over, a lot of words spoken and a lot of dollars spent—it is interesting to speculate for a minute on what it all meant. This morning's Gallup Poll showed President Johnson ahead by almost two-to-one. The interesting thing is that the week after the Republican Convention in San Francisco, the Gallup Poll showed almost exactly the same thing. This is not to say the poll is, or has been, or will be totally accurate. We'll find out tomorrow night, when the votes come in. But whether it's right or wrong—in spite of all the speeches, and the midnight airplane flights, and all the fish fries and high school bands, and the spending of 25 million dollars—since San Francisco, the poll hasn't changed. Other evidence, found in interviews around the country, is that great numbers of people decided back in July how they were going to vote, and they have seen or heard nothing since then to change their minds. On that basis, if you ask what all the campaigning has meant, the answer seems to be—very little.

THE NATION VOTES

On Tuesday, November 3, some 70 million citizens troop to the polls to choose their next President —and, wherever they vote, their attention is drawn to the Southwest where, in Texas and Arizona, two Presidential candidates await the verdict.

NESSEN [NBC Radio from Austin, Tex.]: President Johnson spent this Election Day at the ranch, visiting with friends, resting, and going over some government papers. The President and Mrs. Johnson voted this morning in Johnson City, about 15 miles from their ranch. They were the first two people to drop their ballots into the box. Mr. Johnson has been confident for many weeks that he will defeat Sen. Goldwater. He wants this victory, first of all, as an endorsement of himself and his program so he will feel he is President in his own right, instead of being President because of the accident of President Kennedy's assassination. Second, the President wants to win so that what he considers Sen. Goldwater's dangerous views will be discredited and repudiated, and that what the President considers his own responsible views will be approved. If the President does win, he will go to the Civic Auditorium in Austin tonight to make his victory statement.

MacNEIL [from Scottsdale, Arizona]: Sen. Goldwater was up at 5 o'clock this morning to have a look at the desert dawn. He said he couldn't find anyone to make a speech to, so he called up about 25 radio hams and found out that Election Day weather was fine all over the country. At midmorning he went to cast his vote about a mile from his home, at a school with a view of the desert mountains. Instead of going straight in to vote, as other candidates tend to do, he and Mrs. Goldwater waited in line for over an hour. He spent one and a half minutes in the polling booth, and said afterwards that he had split his ticket. This afternoon, the Senator went for a long walk by himself in the desert, then he spent some time in one of his favorite hobbies, transplanting cactus in his garden. He indicated that he will be philosophical about tonight's result: "Whatever the Lord wants, I can live with it."

On election night, the HUNTLEY-BRINKLEY REPORT begins at 6:30 pm EST, with the program originating from NBC's Election Central in New York. At 6:48 pm, John Chancellor reports.

CHANCELLOR: With two per cent of the precincts reporting across the country in the Presidential race, our calculations show President Johnson as the projected winner of the popular vote. The President is getting 60 to 70 per cent of the popular vote. And let me remind you that in American elections, 60 per cent is a landslide. [The President's eventual percentage is 61.1 per cent.]

It is over very early. Kentucky, Indiana and Kansas are among the first States to report. In Kentucky and Indiana—expected to be close—the President leaps ahead. But the most significant early indicator is traditionally Republican Kansas, where Mr. Johnson gets off to an impressive lead.

Never before is so much of the vote available so early. More than 100,000 reporters mobilized by the Network Election Service—a pooled vote-gathering effort by the broadcasting networks and press services—relay the vote with unprecedented speed. And on election night, NBC presents a remarkably swift and accurate analysis of the 1964 vote by processing this information through its exclusive Election Voting Analysis (EVA) system. [See Tables]

As the reports come in, State after State falls into the President's column. The entire East swings behind Mr. Johnson—including Vermont, which has never before gone Democratic. Across the country, the President's vote surges: he captures every State in the Midwest, all the Plains States, the Mountain States, the entire Pacific Coast. The pattern is clear—Mr. Johnson has won an historic victory by landslide proportions. Of the 50 States, he wins 44, plus the District of Columbia. Sen. Goldwater wins six: his home State of Arizona (narrowly), and five States of the Old Confederacy—Mississippi (where he gets a surprising 87.1% of the vote), Alabama (where the President is not on the ballot), Georgia (which goes Republican for the first time ever), South Carolina and Louisiana. The President piles up 486 electoral votes, to 52 for Sen. Goldwater. Not since 1936, when Franklin D. Roosevelt defeated Alfred Landon (523-8), has there been such an

electoral rout. *And in the popular vote, President Johnson is given a plurality of more than 15 million votes, the biggest margin in the nation's history. Further, the President exhibits great power in pulling in his Party's candidates with him. The Democrats add 38 seats in the House of Representatives, giving them 295 to the Republicans' 140. And they add two seats in the Senate, where their 68 to 32 majority is the heaviest in a quarter of a century. All across the country, Republicans in Congress, State legislatures and local office are swept out in the President's landslide.*

The President wins heavy backing from virtually every group, but his support is almost unanimous among Negroes: 96% in the North, 98% in the Deep South, and 99% in the West. On the other hand, the anticipated "white backlash" vote seems not to materialize. Even localities that supported Alabama Governor George Wallace in the primaries, vote for President Johnson. But the "frontlash"—President Johnson's word for Republicans who vote Democratic—does develop. Heavily Republican areas across the country go Democratic for the first time.

Only unprecedented ticket-splitting saves many prominent moderate Republicans. In Michigan, Gov. Romney survives, running more than 700,000 votes ahead of Sen. Goldwater. Rhode Island's Gov. Chafee is reelected, running 42 per cent ahead of the Senator. In many other States, Republicans are returned to office by running far in front of Sen. Goldwater. But even monumental ticket-splitting fails to save two Republican hopefuls who had captured the attention of the nation: Ohio's Robert Taft Jr., who fails in his bid for the Senate, although he runs 435,000 votes ahead of Sen. Goldwater; and Charles Percy, who fails to win the Governorship of Illinois, although he gets 335,000 more votes than does Sen. Goldwater. The Parties switch Senate seats in New York and California. Robert Kennedy wins in New York over the Republican incumbent, Kenneth Keating; and in California, Republican George Murphy unseats Pierre Salinger.

Only in the Governorships do the Republicans advance. By winning in Washington, Wisconsin and Massachusetts, while losing in Arizona and Utah, they gain one.

On election night in Arizona, it has been expected that Sen. Goldwater would make a statement, but an aide announces that the Senator will not have anything to say until the following morning.

Although the Senator has not conceded, President Johnson goes to Austin's Civic Auditorium as planned, to address his cheering supporters and the nation.

PRESIDENT JOHNSON: We have voted as many, but tonight we must face the world as one...Our purpose must be to bind up our wounds, to heal our history, and to make this nation whole...It is a mandate for unity, for a government that serves no special interest...[Ours] will be a government that provides equal opportunity for all and special privilege for none...I promise the best that is in me for as long as I'm permitted to serve.

O*n Wednesday morning, Nov. 4, Sen. Goldwater holds a news conference. Following are highlights of his statement.*

SEN. GOLDWATER: I have waited until now to make any statement about this election, because I wanted to find out more of the details of the vote...I know many of you expected me to make some statement last night, but I have held off. I have sent the President the following wire:

"Congratulations on your victory. I will help you in any way that I can toward achieving a growing and better America and a secure and dignified peace. The role of the Republican Party will remain in that temper, but it also remains the Party of opposition when opposition is called for. There is much to be done with Vietnam, Cuba, the problem of law and order in this country, and a productive economy. Communism remains our number one obstacle to peace, and I know that all Americans will join you in honest solutions to these problems."

I have no bitterness or rancor at all. I say to the President, as a fellow politician, that he did a wonderful job...I want to express my gratitude to the more than 25 million people...who...voted for a philosophy that I represent, a Republican philosophy that I believe the Republican Party must cling to and strengthen in the years ahead... There is a two-party system in this country, and we are going to keep it...This effort that we engaged in last January 3 turned out to be a much longer effort than we thought. It is not an effort that we can drop now, nor do we have any intention of dropping it now...I will have a lot of time to devote to this Party, to its leadership, and to the strengthening of the Party, and that I have every intention of doing.

CAPTIONS

EPILOGUE

BY CHET HUNTLEY

The American election year was marred by too-recent tragedy; too much vulgarity and meanness; too little nobility and inspiration.

But the continuity of the system by which we govern ourselves remains intact. There may have been anxiety about the choice the people might make. But choice there would be, and choice there was; and the continuity of government would survive. More than 70 million citizens voted for some 10 to 12 thousand candidates for all levels of office. The process would not be interrupted by coup, revolution, ukase, or decree; nor would it be impaired by citizen disinterest or boycott.

There was no precise "opening day" for the political events of 1964. We noted at the beginning of 1963 that political talk was becoming somewhat more acerbic, that there seemed to be some jockeying for position at the starting lines.

We played the guessing-game in which President John F. Kennedy was variously pitted against Gov. Nelson Rockefeller, Richard Nixon, Gov. William Scranton, or Gov. George Romney. Sen. Barry Goldwater was sometimes suggested.

Then, one November afternoon, three rifle shots from a Dallas window numbed a powerful nation. An obscure, self-tortured nobody, in some hallucinated reach for a moment of importance, wrenched the affairs of a planet. The poison of hate-groups and organized social malcontents may have afflicted the brain of this human cipher and turned him into a cataclysmic destroyer. In seven seconds he wrote his piece of history and terminated a hopeful era. The world, through tears, watched in disbelief as the horror was compounded and

211

played out. But there was one reassuring note in the tragic-opera score of that bitter November weekend: without discernible pause, the administrative machinery of our government responded to new management.

There followed a well-advised hiatus of political activity, but shortly after the new year we began to turn our attention toward the political processes which could neither be delayed nor put aside. Sen. Goldwater declared himself a candidate for the Republican nomination. So did Gov. Rockefeller, and Sen. Margaret Chase Smith, and the pathetic victim of political ill-fate, perennial Harold Stassen. Richard Nixon also entered the lists, vainly attempting to disguise his bid as a polite response to a draft movement emanating from somewhere in the hills of New Hampshire. With somewhat more finesse, a draft movement in behalf of Ambassador Henry Cabot Lodge, United States Ambassador to South Vietnam, was launched in the New Hampshire primary—a development which the Ambassador did not disavow and which was energetically directed by his son.

Underdog Winners

Ambassador Lodge proved to be the choice of New Hampshire's Republicans. In May, Oregon's Republicans chose Gov. Rockefeller. In early June, California's Republican voters served notice that the nomination of Sen. Goldwater was an accomplished fact, as they chose him over the New York Governor. Mr. Rockefeller told newsmen that the birth of his son a few nights before the California primary probably cost him the election, since it drew attention to his recent divorce and remarriage. The polls had given the Governor the lead. Of such subtle factors great political decisions are often made.

The California primary eliminated all but the most stubborn doubt:

Goldwater had the delegates. There was a belated flurry in behalf of Gov. Scranton of Pennsylvania which was to surrender ignominiously at the Republican National Convention.

Organization Men

How was it that a candidate who had won only a single well-contested primary could sweep the Convention? This performance went far beyond that of the Kennedy pre-Convention "organization" four years earlier. John F. Kennedy had won several primaries, including the seriously contested trials in Wisconsin and West Virginia. Key men in the Goldwater "organization" were most candid in explaining the technique. They had started in 1960. They went to the precincts and counties and legislative districts of the nation in search of Goldwater delegates to the 1964 Convention. Some they won by persuasion. Some were, by conviction, already there. Others had to be coached, cajoled, or otherwise persuaded to join the right party organization, to attend the significant meetings, to stay at the meetings longer than the opposition, to get the resolutions adopted, and the Goldwater delegates chosen. It required planning, work and money.

Here, indeed, was something relatively new in American politics. Organizational skill and money had taken the nominating prerogative out of the control of the national Convention. At this moment, it is uncertain whether the nominating procedure will return to a mixture of open Convention and delegates elected by primary contest. If the political Convention continues to be denied its nominating prerogative, more States may adopt the Presidential primary.

The San Francisco Republican Convention was, in effect, a microcosm of a sizeable, inarticulate bloc of the American electorate. The delegates

rejected the premise that the individual living in a twentieth century industrial society might require occasional assistance in coping with the complications of that society. They harbored a nostalgia for the sweet innocence of America's youthful era, the frontier society with its simplicity, its individualism, its moral code.

The delegates frequently identified those responsible for the loss of military invincibility, for softness toward communism, for government spending, for "creeping socialism," moral decay, and government graft and favoritism only as "they." The implication was, however, that "they" were Democrats and Eastern, liberal Republicans. These groups had been managing the country for 30 years, and look at the shape it was in.

Triumphant Protest

The Republican Convention represented a protest of uncertain proportion. As protest movements usually are, this one was inarticulate and imprecise. It had been ignored in previous election years, disavowed by Dewey, Eisenhower, Nixon, Rockefeller, Lodge and the others. Its one-time favorite, Gen. Douglas MacArthur, had been rejected. Now, Sen. Barry Goldwater had not only accepted the protest movement, but had given it status and respectability by appearing to be part of it.

The protest movement owned the Convention and would brook no compromise with its adversaries. Southern delegations were lily-white to a degree unmatched in this century, but what of it? The moderate opposition, belatedly coalescing around Gov. Scranton, demanded a disavowal of the John Birch Society and other extremist groups in the platform, but it was spurned. A carefully-worded compromise offered by Gov. Romney was howled down; Gov. Rockefeller was overwhelmed by roars of deri-

sion. A proposal that the platform pledge support for the Negro civil rights movement and stern enforcement of the new Civil Rights Act was buried in an avalanche of "noes." In his acceptance speech, the nominee declared extremism a virtue, and he invited his adversaries and critics within the Party to go elsewhere. As a final back-of-the-hand gesture, Goldwater selected the comparatively obscure New York Congressman and Republican National Chairman, William Miller, as his running mate.

The New Breed

This was the Republican Convention of 1964, and these were its participants. The majority of the delegates were attending their first Convention. They were members of the hitherto disregarded protest movement mobilized by Sen. Goldwater, and his task force. In utter frustration, Henry Cabot Lodge said, "Who are these people? I've never seen any of them before!" Familiar faces and names were missing. Several State governors were denied places in their delegations for failure to join the Goldwater movement. The delegates were brash, intemperate, and quick to anger. They shook their fists at the journalists. In restaurants, hotel lobbies, and elevators they accosted newsmen, angrily asserting that Goldwater was the victim of a massive plot to make him look ridiculous and inept.

There was new money at the Convention and in the Goldwater campaign: money from Texas, Southern California, Colorado, Arizona, and the South. It had not the patina of quiet reserve and dignity of the traditional Republican money from Wall Street, Pittsburgh's Golden Triangle, or the Union League Club of Philadelphia.

In the background and on the Convention fringes were the captains of organized extremist groups. They were the outriders, attempting to guide the general direction of the protest congress; urging no compromise with the "effete" Republicans of the East; demanding complete humiliation of "the creeping socialists," "the starry-eyed do-gooders," "the bleeding hearts," "the me-tooists," "the Little Sir Echoes."

Extremist literature was dispensed by the ton and extremist recruiting did a brisk business.

Both the mood and the substance of the Convention skirted the fragile boundaries of racism, portending a campaign which cautiously probed at that dark and foreboding area.

The Republican Party, hostage of the protest movement and sanctuary of the extremists, had insured the worst defeat in history; but it would still garner twenty-six million votes!

The Democrats, confident of a victory, experimented with a late Convention. They assembled late in August in Atlantic City with one sticky problem and one unknown decision. Their problem involved the seating of Southern delegates who had let it be known that they would oppose or withhold support from the Party's ticket. The unknown was President Johnson's choice for the Vice Presidential nomination.

Mississippi Struggle

A significant struggle developed over a challenge to the Mississippi delegation. It was a white delegation, and it appeared to have bona-fide status in that it had met the qualifications of Mississippi State law.

It was challenged, however, by a second Mississippi delegation, virtually all Negro, counseled and directed by an alliance of Northern civil rights organizations. Members of the challenging delegation, or "Freedom Delegation," as it was called, shocked the Convention with their testimony revealing persecution and even torture at the hands of whites in Mississippi who were determined to bar the Negro from political action.

However, the Freedom Delegation, for all its moral claim, did lack legal status. The laws of Mississippi governing the selection of Convention delegates were patently unfair and were obviously calculated to maintain the lily-white character of the State's delegation; but the Freedom Group had failed to meet the requirements. And the Convention had no jurisdiction over Mississippi laws.

A Precedent Established

As a compromise, the Convention offered the Freedom Delegation a token vote and a token place on the Convention floor. The white delegation walked out of the Convention and returned home. The Negro group —enthusiastic over the reception given it, but inexperienced in the art of political compromise—rejected the token offer, demanding total victory on one ballot or in one motion. However, the Democratic Convention established a committee to assist Mississippi Negroes in their efforts to enter the Democratic Party of that State and to vote freely for delegates to the next Convention.

This episode in the Democratic Convention was one of the meaningful events of the political year.

The Mississippi Freedom Delegation had been well-counseled. They had shaved off beards, they wore neckties and jackets, there would be no "sitting-in," no demonstrations. They had come a long way, and they discovered that there was a recourse in the political arena—in a Convention and at the ballot box.

The Democrats wrote and adopted a platform which pointed with pride to the Civil Rights Act of 1964 and condemned the Communist Party, the Ku Klux Klan, the John Birch Society, and similar organizations.

President Johnson, at virtually the

last excruciating moment, let it be known that his choice for the Vice Presidential nomination was Sen. Hubert Humphrey of Minnesota. It was a popular choice.

The campaign that followed was desultory, irrelevant, and superficial. It altered no opinion; it contained no substantive debate; it offered no profound analysis of where we were or where we might be headed.

Sen. Goldwater and Rep. Miller charged their opponents with hypocrisy, graft, corruption, stupidity, immorality, power-seeking and assorted other sins; but the indictments lacked conviction and documentation. They were delivered in weary rote. Conservatism was lost, unmentioned, unexplained—Goldwater either deserted it or never did really mean it. He continued to leap from one epigram to another and then squander time and public patience trying to explain what he had meant. He attempted to establish that he would be the implacable adversary of implacable communism, but then he had to contend with the impression that he might be unstable and inclined to march backward from action to judgment. He appeared to reject Sam Rayburn's simple formula for great Presidents: "Men who know how to say, 'Just a minute!'" The latter stage of the Goldwater-Miller campaign took on the tone of a moral crusade.

Presidential Goals

President Johnson was never really challenged to defend his policies and plans, domestic or foreign. He talked about "the Great Society," the need for more and finer education, medical care for the aged and more opportunity for all segments of the nation. Sometimes it seemed that the two candidates were competing for different offices.

Sen. Humphrey brought additional substance to the campaign. He talked about civil rights and full citizenship, about big government, and the lack of answers to imponderable questions. His audiences listened.

The Republican loss in the Senate was a modest two seats, but it was a staggering thirty-eight in the House of Representatives, and more than five hundred in the fifty State legislatures! The Republican Party was in jeopardy. In the majority of the States, Democratic-controlled legislatures would, by order of the United States Supreme Court, redraw State legislative districts by 1966. The reapportionment would give the Republicans no comfort.

Picking Up the Pieces

However, the G.O.P. had gained one governorship. The reconstruction of the Party would have to be given to some powerful vote-getters who had survived the Democratic avalanche: Rep. Lindsay of New York; Governors Romney of Michigan, Evans of Washington, and Chafee of Rhode Island; and to men who were not on the 1964 ballot—among them Governors Rockefeller, Hatfield, and Scranton; and Senators Javits, Kuchel, Scott, Carlson, Cooper, and others such as Richard M. Nixon.

As the Republican Party surveyed its wreckage, there was no conclusive evaluation of our political bill of health. The protest movement and the extremists were not about to disperse or relax their claim on the Grand Old Party. They pointed to twenty-six million votes and challenged traditional and responsible Republicans to find twenty-six million votes anywhere else. How could the Republican Party husband that strength and simultaneously take nine or ten million votes away from the Democrats? The license of a political party is an occasional victory.

The protest movement will require attention. It cannot be permitted to wander about in political limbo. It must not be the hunting ground for demagogues. Democrats, Republicans, independents, and private study groups might conclude that the twenty-six million bloc requires attention. Its anxieties must be ameliorated, its anger assuaged, and its trust in democratic processes enhanced. To be sure, the Goldwater vote was not made up of twenty-six million nuts or neurotics; nor can it be rationalized away by deducting the Southern segregationist vote, the solid Republican vote, or the anti-Johnson vote.

The six-and-a-half-million votes in the five Southern States which went Republican were part of the protest movement. Whether the election left us with a valid two-Party system in the South is not certain. The Republican Party cannot be segregationist in Dixie and anti-segregationist in the North. The votes of the five Goldwater States of the South are important and they are tempting, but can they serve as the foundation upon which to reconstruct a major national Party? It is folly to believe that the South will elect to remain forever outside the main current of American political thought and action. The cost of separatism is too high.

The Negro Gain

The American Negro, almost totally, identified his aspirations with the Democratic Party and he may stay there for some time. This past election year may be said to have been the one in which the Negro made his most meaningful gains of the past century. The Federal government, by act of Congress, now was committed to the elimination of many forms of segregation and discrimination involving overt acts; the Democratic Party was pledged to help him participate at all levels of Party business; the Democratic Party was aware that the Negro vote had clearly

brought Florida, Virginia and, possibly, Arkansas into the Johnson column on election day; and the feared civil rights backlash had significant proportions in only five Southern States. Lyndon Johnson's defeat in the five Southern States lay in the narrow belt of one hundred rural counties, each with significant Negro populations or Negro majorities who were unable to vote, and each the sure target of future Negro registration drives.

It may be doubted that 1964 marked a "Custer's last stand" for the nostalgic pull of a return to our frontier innocence. The folklore of its simplicity will linger on.

Perhaps our educators will ultimately decide to reckon with the hunger for answers to every problem. Is our education process placing undue stress on two and two yielding four, and too little on the appreciation of imponderables? What honor is given in our classrooms to that delightful phrase, "I don't know"?

We learned that political parties are not immune to infiltration and capture. The Democrats learned that hard lesson in the late 30's and 40's. The lunatic fringe is employing the Republican Party as its host-institution, like a spore settling upon the host-plant for sustenance and propagation. The extremists seized upon the protest movement, infected it, and offered it to the Republican Party.

The Unlearned Lesson

The election year taught us little or nothing about American conservatism; whether it is a valid concept, a meaningless cliche or a mirage. We still have no precise way of knowing what popular demand or acceptance there might have been for a constructive, conservative Presidential candidate proposing a program of modest social change rather than a program of nihilism in which the clocks would be made to run backward. We are left to hope that responsible political leaders, and the rank and file as well, discovered anew that this nation deserves better than a choice between extremes.

The Real Questions

Does valid American conservatism include a persistent questioning of the Federal government's role as regulator and referee of the nation's commerce; stabilizer and catalyst of the national economy; prime source of social welfare; giant builder, and chief revenue collector and dispenser?

Does constructive American conservatism ask a "show-cause" in instances where government authority or activity may be intruding into the private sector or needlessly undermining the prerogatives of the States?

Does conservatism call for a dispassionate examination of every phase of public social welfare in a clear effort to reduce its multi-billion-dollar proportions and preclude its self-perpetuation?

Does responsible conservatism include some concern about the danger of an ultimate alliance between government and industry in a pact of home-grown national socialism?

Does conservatism embody concern about Federal regulatory authority carried to the excess of a kind of fascism or syndicalism?

Does conservatism mean a healthy wedding of economic and social planning to a responsible laissez-faire profit motive?

Does conservatism make a distinction between the Russian people and the Soviet government, and can it make clear that we want nothing from the Russian people which is rightfully theirs—including their government?

Does American conservatism reserve the hope that the communist adversary may change his tactics, if not his ultimate objectives, because of the harsh realities of planetary nuclear holocaust and the stresses of economic necessity?

Does conservatism include in its manifesto some appeal to the American intellectual and a corresponding rejection of the grandchildren of Mencken's "boobs"?

If constructive American conservatism means these things, and others, then it had no hearing in last year's election processes; and it, as well as the nation, suffered a grievous injury.

Perhaps we learned something in 1964 about the growing sophistication of the American voter, for he broke every known world record in ballot-splitting. The prime example, perhaps, was in New York's 17th Congressional District, where Johnson achieved a record majority but where Republican Congressman John Lindsay became one of the biggest individual winners of all the Congressional, gubernatorial, and Senate candidates in the United States. Politicians are not enthusiastic about ballot-splitting, and so it remains to be seen whether they will try to make it more difficult.

The Unanswered Questions

There were some hopeful suggestions for shorter campaigns, which will probably be forgotten by Labor Day of 1968.

Yet, all these forces, fears and folktales must be taken into account. That was the lesson of 1964.

The Democratic Party may have won too easily for it to look to the storm warnings. It can live happily on its new endowment of unmatched political victory and swollen majorities.

But twenty-six million votes are still somehow unaccounted for. We do not know how they were divided among classic Republicans, segregationists, "Johnson-phobes," desperate conservatives, and radical nuts. Altogether, however, they are the American protest movement—the coalition of discontent.

215

1964 ELECTION RETURNS

The vote totals shown in chart A are based on complete, official vote totals reported by State government sources. The vote figures in charts B-I were compiled by the newly formed Network Election Service, as of 9:00 pm, EST, Wednesday, November 4. Network Election Service represented the pooled efforts of the broadcasting networks and the press services in gathering vote totals throughout the nation.

Through the work of the NES, the nation saw the election results earlier than ever before in history.

While the vote totals shown in the NES charts are unofficial, they reflect a clear picture of the nation's voting patterns. The totals here include all but a few scattered returns which—at the time this volume went to press—were not available because 1) some States delayed reporting the votes of outlying districts, 2) some did not count absentee ballots immediately and, 3) several areas were still contesting ballots.

(A) 1964 PRESIDENTIAL ELECTION RESULTS

STATE	ELECTORAL VOTE JOHN-SON	ELECTORAL VOTE GOLD-WATER	POPULAR VOTE JOHN-SON	POPULAR VOTE GOLD-WATER	DEMO-CRATIC PER-CENTAGE	REPUB-LICAN PER-CENTAGE
*ALABAMA		10		479,085		69.5
ALASKA	3		44,329	22,930	65.9	34.1
ARIZONA		5	237,753	242,535	49.7	50.1
ARKANSAS	6		314,197	243,265	56.1	43.4
CALIFORNIA	40		4,171,877	2,879,108	59.2	40.8
COLORADO	6		476,024	296,767	61.3	38.2
CONNECTICUT	8		826,269	390,996	67.8	32.1
DELAWARE	3		122,704	78,078	60.9	38.8
DIST. OF COLUMBIA	3		169,796	28,801	85.5	14.5
FLORIDA	14		948,540	905,941	51.1	48.9
GEORGIA		12	522,557	616,584	45.9	54.1
HAWAII	4		163,249	44,022	78.8	22.1
IDAHO	4		148,920	143,557	50.9	49.1
ILLINOIS	26		2,796,833	1,905,946	59.5	40.5
INDIANA	13		1,170,848	911,118	56.0	43.6
IOWA	9		733,030	449,148	61.9	37.9
KANSAS	7		464,028	386,579	54.1	45.1
KENTUCKY	9		669,659	372,977	64.0	35.7
LOUISIANA		10	387,068	509,225	43.2	56.8
MAINE	4		262,264	118,701	68.8	31.2
MARYLAND	10		730,912	385,495	65.5	34.5
MASSACHUSETTS	14		1,786,422	549,727	76.2	23.5
MICHIGAN	21		2,136,615	1,060,152	66.8	33.2
MINNESOTA	10		991,117	559,624	63.8	36.0
MISSISSIPPI		7	52,618	356,528	12.9	87.1
MISSOURI	12		1,164,344	635,535	64.0	36.0
MONTANA	4		164,246	113,032	58.9	40.6
NEBRASKA	5		307,307	276,847	52.6	47.4
NEVADA	3		79,339	56,094	58.6	41.4
NEW HAMPSHIRE	4		182,065	104,029	63.6	36.4
NEW JERSEY	17		1,867,671	963,843	65.6	33.9
NEW MEXICO	4		194,017	131,838	59.2	40.2
NEW YORK	43		4,913,156	2,243,559	68.6	31.3
NORTH CAROLINA	13		800,139	624,844	56.2	43.8
NORTH DAKOTA	4		149,784	108,207	58.0	41.9
OHIO	26		2,498,331	1,470,865	62.9	37.1
OKLAHOMA	8		519,834	412,665	55.7	44.3
OREGON	6		501,017	282,779	63.8	36.0
PENNSYLVANIA	29		3,130,236	1,672,923	65.0	34.7
RHODE ISLAND	4		315,463	74,615	80.9	19.1
SOUTH CAROLINA		8	215,700	309,048	41.1	58.9
SOUTH DAKOTA	4		163,010	130,108	55.6	44.4
TENNESSEE	11		635,047	508,965	55.5	44.5
TEXAS	25		1,663,185	958,566	63.3	36.5
UTAH	4		219,628	180,682	54.9	45.1
VERMONT	3		108,127	54,942	66.3	33.7
VIRGINIA	12		558,038	481,334	53.5	46.2
WASHINGTON	9		779,699	470,366	62.0	37.4
WEST VIRGINIA	7		538,087	253,953	67.9	32.1
WISCONSIN	12		1,055,424	638,495	62.2	37.6
WYOMING	3		80,718	61,998	56.6	43.4
TOTALS	486	52	43,131,241	27,157,111	61.1	38.5

*Alabama's Democratic Electors were unpledged. Their total vote: 210,732.
Total vote for third parties (including Alabama): 319,315.
This is .4% of the national vote.

(B) 1964 SENATORIAL ELECTION RESULTS

STATE	DEMOCRATIC CANDIDATE	DEMOCRATIC TOTAL	REPUBLICAN CANDIDATE	REPUBLICAN TOTAL	WIN-NING %
ARIZONA	ELSON	213,720	†FANNIN	225,074	51.3
CALIFORNIA	SALINGER	3,188,133	†MURPHY	3,355,565	51.3
CONNECTICUT	†DODD	779,068	LODGE	425,263	64.7
DELAWARE	CARVEL	96,863	†WILLIAMS, J.	103,727	51.7
FLORIDA	†HOLLAND	938,989	KIRK	552,900	62.9
HAWAII	GILL	96,689	†FONG	110,723	53.4
INDIANA	†HARTKE	1,110,930	BONTRAGER	932,552	54.4
MAINE	†MUSKIE	251,605	McINTIRE	126,175	66.6
MARYLAND	†TYDINGS	691,801	BEALL	401,411	63.3
MASSACHUSETTS	†KENNEDY, E.	1,602,015	WHITMORE	552,542	74.4
AMICHIGAN	†HART	1,973,602	PETERSON	1,089,952	64.4
MINNESOTA	†McCARTHY	921,725	WHITNEY	608,174	60.2
MISSOURI	†SYMINGTON	1,116,180	BRADSHAW	538,386	67.5
MONTANA	†MANSFIELD	169,827	BLEWETT	93,485	64.5
NEBRASKA	ARNDT	209,150	†HRUSKA	329,118	61.1
NEVADA	†CANNON	67,302	LAXALT	67,186	50.0
NEW JERSEY	†WILLIAMS, H.	1,651,413	SHANLEY	996,150	62.4
NEW MEXICO	†MONTOYA	177,074	MECHEM	146,768	54.7
BNEW YORK	†KENNEDY, R.	3,800,514	KEATING	3,088,557	53.6
NORTH DAKOTA	†BURDICK	141,002	KLEPPE	104,929	57.3
OHIO	†YOUNG	1,920,085	TAFT	1,907,011	50.2
OKLAHOMA	†HARRIS	468,064	WILKINSON	443,940	51.3
PENNSYLVANIA	BLATT	2,296,703	†SCOTT	2,349,694	50.6
RHODE ISLAND	†PASTORE	307,993	LAGUEUX	63,889	82.8
TENNESSEE	†GORE	570,703	KUYKENDALL	494,185	53.6
	†BASS	570,445	BAKER	518,097	52.4
TEXAS	†YARBOROUGH	1,435,315	BUSH	1,110,270	56.4
UTAH	†MOSS	228,210	WILKINSON	169,492	57.4
VERMONT	FAYETTE	76,517	†PROUTY	87,441	53.3
CVIRGINIA	†BYRD, H.	588,737	MAY	172,749	69.0
WASHINGTON	†JACKSON	793,485	ANDREWS	305,323	72.2
WEST VIRGINIA	†BYRD, R.	509,202	BENEDICT	244,439	67.5
WISCONSIN	†PROXMIRE	867,365	RENK	759,901	53.3
WYOMING	†McGEE	73,547	WOLD	63,220	53.8

†WINNING CANDIDATE
ATHIRD PARTY (SMITH—FREEDOM NOW)—3,003
BTHIRD PARTY (PAOLUCCI—CONSERVATIVE)—203,369
CTHIRD PARTY (RESPESS—INDEPENDENT)—91,281

(C) SENATE COMPOSITION BY PARTY

	1964 D	1964 R	Change D	Change R	1962 D	1962 R	1960 D	1960 R	1958 D	1958 R	1956 D	1956 R
NORTH	19	11	+1	—1	18	12	14	16	15	15	8	22
ELECTED	10	3			6	4	3	5	9	4	2	7
HOLDOVERS	9	8			12	8	11	11	6	11	6	15
SOUTH	28	4	0	0	28	4	28	4	28	4	27	5
ELECTED	10	0			10	2	13	1	9	1	10	4
HOLDOVERS	18	4			18	2	15	3	19	3	17	1
WEST	21	17	0	0	21	17	22	16	21	15	14	20
ELECTED	8	4			8	9	7	8	10	3	6	6
HOLDOVERS	13	13			13	8	15	8	11	12	8	14
NATION	68	32	+1	—1	67	33	64	36	64	34	49	47
ELECTED	28	7			24	15	23	14	28	8	18	17
HOLDOVERS	40	25			43	18	41	22	36	26	31	30

(Continued)

(D) SENATE COMPOSITION BY ISSUES*

	Senators Who Favor	Change From '62	Senators Who Oppose	Change From '62	No Stand	Change From '62
MEDICARE BILL	54	+2	45	—2	1	0
POVERTY PROGRAM	65	+1	34	—2	1	+1
TEST-BAN TREATY	82	+1	18	—1	0	0
CLOTURE	72	+1	27	—2	1	+1
MASS TRANSIT BILL	53	—1	43	—2	4	+2

*Based on stands taken by the winning candidates

(E) 1964 GUBERNATORIAL ELECTION RESULTS

STATE	DEMOCRATIC CANDIDATE	TOTAL	REPUBLICAN CANDIDATE	TOTAL	WINNING %
ARIZONA	†GODDARD	237,184	KLEINDIENST	207,290	53.4
ARKANSAS	†FAUBUS	294,042	ROCKEFELLER	217,459	57.5
DELAWARE	†TERRY	102,803	BUCKSON	97,145	51.4
FLORIDA	†BURNS	876,633	HOLLEY	652,340	57.3
ILLINOIS	†KERNER	2,386,502	PERCY	2,211,338	51.9
INDIANA	†BRANIGIN	1,153,284	RISTIN	892,438	56.4
IOWA	†HUGHES	791,067	HULTMAN	362,891	68.6
KANSAS	WILES	329,827	†AVERY	376,309	53.3
MASSACHUSETTS	BELLOTTI	1,091,022	†VOLPE	1,111,417	50.5
*MICHIGAN	STAEBLER	1,369,254	†ROMNEY	1,764,542	56.2
MISSOURI	†HEARNES	1,044,853	SHEPLEY	642,615	61.9
MONTANA	RENNE	130,812	†BABCOCK	137,687	51.3
NEBRASKA	†MORRISON	332,299	BURNEY	222,051	59.9
NEW HAMPSHIRE	†KING	190,782	PILLSBURY	94,901	66.8
NEW MEXICO	†CAMPBELL	191,185	TUCKER	126,722	60.1
NORTH CAROLINA	†MOORE	777,136	GAVIN	603,526	56.3
NORTH DAKOTA	†GUY	137,673	HALCROW	109,385	55.7
RHODE ISLAND	GALLOGLY	146,201	†CHAFEE	231,888	61.3
SOUTH DAKOTA	LINDLEY	140,254	†BOE	147,738	51.3
TEXAS	†CONNALLY	1,832,102	CRICHTON	697,256	72.4
UTAH	†RAMPTON	227,051	MELICH	171,395	57.0
VERMONT	†HOFF	106,689	FOOTE	57,728	64.9
WASHINGTON	ROSELLINI	491,994	†EVANS	630,508	56.2
WEST VIRGINIA	†SMITH	428,976	UNDERWOOD	353,857	54.8
WISCONSIN	REYNOLDS	815,484	†KNOWLES	833,806	50.6

*THIRD PARTY (CLEAGE—FREEDOM NOW)—3,288   †WINNING CANDIDATE

(F) GUBERNATORIAL SUMMARY BY PARTY

	1964 D	1964 R	Change D	Change R	1962 D	1962 R	1960 D	1960 R	1958 D	1958 R	1956 D	1956 R
NORTH	7	8	—2	+2	9	6	10	5	8	7	8	7
SOUTH	15	1	0	0	15	1	16	0	15	1	14	2
WEST	11	8	+1	—1	10	9	8	11	12	6	8	9
NATION	33	17	—1	+1	34	16	34	16	35	14	30	18

(G) HOUSE ELECTION RESULTS

STATE	DEMOCRATIC CANDIDATE	TOTAL	REPUBLICAN CANDIDATE	TOTAL	WINNING %
ALABAMA					
CONG. DIST. 1	TYSON	37,472	†EDWARDS	59,282	61.3
CONG. DIST. 2	GRANT	24,086	†DICKINSON	40,428	62.7
CONG. DIST. 3	ANDREWS		No Republican candidate		
CONG. DIST. 4	ROBERTS	26,301	†ANDREWS	35,538	57.5
CONG. DIST. 5	†SELDEN	40,099	FRENCH	33,955	54.1
CONG. DIST. 6	HUDDLESTON	44,255	†BUCHANAN	72,659	62.1
CONG. DIST. 7	HAWKINS	41,350	†MARTIN	61,634	59.8
CONG. DIST. 8	JONES		No Republican candidate		
ALASKA					
AT LARGE	†RIVERS	30,466	THOMAS	29,991	50.4
ARIZONA					
CONG. DIST. 1	AHEARN	111,130	†RHODES	135,729	55.0
CONG. DIST. 2	†UDALL	81,615	KIMBLE	55,460	59.5
CONG. DIST. 3	†SENNER	30,503	STEIGER	28,708	57.5
ARKANSAS					
CONG. DIST. 1	GATHINGS		No Republican Candidate		
CONG. DIST. 2	MILLS		No Republican Candidate		
CONG. DIST. 3	†TRIMBLE	61,997	HINSHAW	52,559	54.1
CONG. DIST. 4	HARRIS		No Republican Candidate		
CALIFORNIA					
CONG. DIST. 1	McCABE	84,877	†CLAUSEN	117,378	58.0
CONG. DIST. 2	†JOHNSON	115,363	MERRIAM	63,857	64.4
CONG. DIST. 3	†MOSS	159,256	GJELSTEEN	55,085	74.3
CONG. DIST. 4	†LEGGETT	84,902	NORRIS	33,231	71.9
CONG. DIST. 5	BURTON		No Republican candidate		
CONG. DIST. 6	O'TOOLE	69,604	†MAILLIARD	120,062	63.3
CONG. DIST. 7	†COHELAN	100,050	McNUTT	50,075	66.6
CONG. DIST. 8	†MILLER	107,714	McKAY	45,734	70.2
CONG. DIST. 9	†EDWARDS	112,275	HYDE	48,701	69.3
CONG. DIST. 10	CARMAN	85,599	†GUBSER	144,439	62.8
CONG. DIST. 11	SULLIVAN	90,164	†YOUNGER	106,726	54.2
CONG. DIST. 12	BOLZ	60,086	†TALCOTT	97,928	61.9
CONG. DIST. 13	TAYLOR	77,937	†TEAGUE	104,643	57.3
CONG. DIST. 14	KOCH	62,956	†BALDWIN	116,108	64.8
CONG. DIST. 15	†McFALL	109,514	GIBSON	44,962	70.9
CONG. DIST. 16	†SISK	117,085	HARRIS	55,476	67.9
CONG. DIST. 17	†KING	59,811	MUNCASTER	47,624	55.7
CONG. DIST. 18	†HAGEN	114,664	WILLIAMS	56,920	66.8
CONG. DIST. 19	†HOLIFIELD	63,513	HUNT	26,459	70.6
CONG. DIST. 20	KAUFMAN	68,553	†SMITH	147,698	68.3
CONG. DIST. 21	†HAWKINS	97,378	LUNDY	14,053	87.4
CONG. DIST. 22	†CORMAN	90,986	CLINE	86,007	51.4
CONG. DIST. 23	VAN PETTEN	67,808	†CLAWSON	81,345	54.5
CONG. DIST. 24	STEVENS	54,303	†LIPSCOMB	108,732	66.7
CONG. DIST. 25	†CAMERON	66,080	WALTON	52,574	55.7
CONG. DIST. 26	†ROOSEVELT	114,004	SETON	49,060	69.9
CONG. DIST. 27	BANE	81,186	†REINECKE	89,684	52.5
CONG. DIST. 28	GOTTLIEB	93,728	†BELL	173,180	64.9
CONG. DIST. 29	†BROWN	76,755	FARRINGTON	53,863	58.3
CONG. DIST. 30	†ROYBAL	84,131	FEDER	37,821	69.0
CONG. DIST. 31	†WILSON	102,201	SHANAHAN	59,436	63.2
CONG. DIST. 32	CULLEN	28,653	†HOSMER	58,368	67.1
CONG. DIST. 33	†DYAL	102,522	PETTIS	95,337	51.8
CONG. DIST. 34	†HANNA	81,270	GEIER	56,450	59.0
CONG. DIST. 35	CARPENTER	63,097	†UTT	123,623	66.2
CONG. DIST. 36	WHELAN	41,363	†WILSON	58,188	58.5
CONG. DIST. 37	†VAN DEERLIN	35,875	WILSON	26,235	57.8
CONG. DIST. 38	†TUNNEY	75,853	MARTIN	65,731	53.6
COLORADO					
CONG. DIST. 1	†ROGERS	138,475	JONES	65,422	67.9
CONG. DIST. 2	†McVICKER	108,531	BROTZMAN	105,261	50.8
CONG. DIST. 3	†EVANS	85,382	CHENOWETH	81,470	51.2
CONG. DIST. 4	†ASPINALL	106,312	LAMM	62,731	62.9
CONNECTICUT					
CONG. DIST. 1	†DADDARIO	141,003	COLLINS	60,464	70.0
CONG. DIST. 2	†ONGE	119,036	COPP	69,164	63.3
CONG. DIST. 3	†GIAIMO	124,484	BURNS	69,373	64.2
CONG. DIST. 4	†IRWIN	117,090	SIBAL	108,202	52.0
CONG. DIST. 5	†MONAGAN	131,025	TERRELL	63,981	67.2
CONG. DIST. 6	†GRABOWSKI	114,793	MESKILL	80,921	58.7
DELAWARE					
AT LARGE	†McDOWELL	111,370	SNOWDEN	85,345	56.6
FLORIDA					
CONG. DIST. 1	SIKES		No Republican candidate		
CONG. DIST. 2	†BENNETT	93,991	STOCKTON	35,630	72.5
CONG. DIST. 3	†PEPPER	88,382	O'NEILL	46,128	65.7
CONG. DIST. 4	†FASCELL	94,944	McGLON	52,170	64.5
CONG. DIST. 5	HERLONG		No Republican candidate		
CONG. DIST. 6	†ROGERS	155,214	STEELE	79,431	66.1
CONG. DIST. 7	HALEY		No Republican candidate		

(Continued)

STATE FLORIDA	DEMOCRATIC CANDIDATE	TOTAL	REPUBLICAN CANDIDATE	TOTAL	WIN-NING %
CONG. DIST. 8	MATTHEWS		No Republican candidate		
CONG. DIST. 9	FUQUA		No Republican candidate		
CONG. DIST. 10	GIBBONS		No Republican candidate		
CONG. DIST. 11	KENNEY	59,403	†GURNEY	90,661	60.4
CONG. DIST. 12	HARRELSON	62,521	†CRAMER	93,065	59.8
GEORGIA					
CONG. DIST. 1	†HAGAN	65,146	LENT	25,006	68.5
CONG. DIST. 2	O'NEAL		No Republican candidate		
CONG. DIST. 3	BYRD	33,733	†CALLAWAY	45,145	57.6
CONG. DIST. 4	†MacKAY	66,488	PICKETT	50,326	58.0
CONG. DIST. 5	†WELTNER	65,803	O'CALLAGHAN	55,983	55.1
CONG. DIST. 6	FLYNT		No Republican candidate		
CONG. DIST. 7	†DAVIS	69,575	CHOPIN	57,562	53.4
CONG. DIST. 8	TUTEN		No Republican candidate		
CONG. DIST. 9	†LANDRUM	59,186	PRINCE	38,608	63.5
CONG. DIST. 10	STEPHENS		No Republican candidate		
HAWAII					
AT LARGE	†MATSUNAGA	140,190	SUTTON	56,130	73.0
AT LARGE	†MINK	107,003	MILLIGAN	89,299	55.0
IDAHO					
CONG. DIST. 1	†WHITE	56,203	MATTMILLER	52,468	51.7
CONG. DIST. 2	HARDING	84,022	†HANSEN	91,838	52.2
ILLINOIS					
CONG. DIST. 1	†DAWSON	142,688	DANIEL	25,719	84.7
CONG. DIST. 2	†O'HARA	102,514	SCANNELL	52,687	66.0
CONG. DIST. 3	†MURPHY	116,739	BYRNE	77,963	60.0
CONG. DIST. 4	RYBACKI	70,800	†DERWINSKI	105,805	60.0
CONG. DIST. 5	†KLUCZYNSKI	102,861	KOTOWSKI	56,194	64.7
CONG. DIST. 6	†RONAN	83,635	HALAC	17,390	82.8
CONG. DIST. 7	†ANNUNZIO	102,089	WOLFRAM	19,242	84.1
CONG. DIST. 8	†ROSTENKOWSKI	135,060	EBROM	70,752	65.6
CONG. DIST. 9	†YATES	84,024	DECKER	47,783	63.7
CONG. DIST. 10	GAUSE	106,103	†COLLIER	164,014	60.7
CONG. DIST. 11	†PUCINSKI	125,606	PODGORSKI	94,032	57.2
CONG. DIST. 12	KIMBALL	43,533	†McCLORY	64,843	59.8
CONG. DIST. 13	WILLIAMS	101,796	†RUMSFELD	128,931	55.9
CONG. DIST. 14	ZIEGLER	78,473	†ERLENBORN	111,586	58.7
CONG. DIST. 15	MITCHELL	44,373	†REID	65,194	59.5
CONG. DIST. 16	BRINKMEIER	52,395	†ANDERSON	68,888	56.8
CONG. DIST. 17	HUGHES	63,074	†ARENDS	81,015	56.2
CONG. DIST. 18	KOHLBACHER	60,715	†MICHEL	71,534	54.1
CONG. DIST. 19	†SCHISLER	79,305	McLOSKEY	72,206	52.3
CONG. DIST. 20	COLLINS	98,722	†FINDLEY	118,835	54.6
CONG. DIST. 21	†GRAY	91,968	STANARD	51,146	64.3
CONG. DIST. 22	DESMOND	67,251	†SPRINGER	75,087	52.8
CONG. DIST. 23	†SHIPLEY	105,394	JONES	88,488	54.4
CONG. DIST. 24	†PRICE	83,452	MIRZA	25,114	76.9
INDIANA					
CONG. DIST. 1	†MADDEN	111,850	ENDRES	67,695	62.3
CONG. DIST. 2	RABER	75,869	†HALLECK	85,716	53.0
CONG. DIST. 3	†BRADEMAS	120,620	MILLER	76,235	61.3
CONG. DIST. 4	HOBBS	81,252	†ADAIR	86,462	51.6
CONG. DIST. 5	†ROUSH	114,445	FEIGHNER	93,159	55.1
CONG. DIST. 6	O'LESSKER	71,370	†ROUDEBUSH	83,077	53.8
CONG. DIST. 7	TIPTON	66,270	†BRAY	76,542	53.6
CONG. DIST. 8	†DENTON	103,366	ZION	79,730	56.5
CONG. DIST. 9	†HAMILTON	67,255	WILSON	57,905	53.7
CONG. DIST. 10	DAVIS	86,224	†HARVEY	87,505	50.5
CONG. DIST. 11	†JACOBS	149,531	TABBERT	146,212	50.6
IOWA					
CONG. DIST. 1	†SCHMIDHAUSER	82,846	SCHWENGEL	79,967	50.9
CONG. DIST. 2	†CULVER	96,785	BROMWELL	89,200	52.0
CONG. DIST. 3	PETERSON	83,095	†GROSS	83,425	50.1
CONG. DIST. 4	†BANDSTRA	82,960	KYL	72,196	53.5
CONG. DIST. 5	†SMITH	108,299	GIBSON	46,232	70.1
CONG. DIST. 6	†GREIGG	86,361	SOKOL	75,882	53.2
CONG. DIST. 7	†HANSEN	78,211	JENSEN	67,981	53.5

STATE KANSAS	DEMOCRATIC CANDIDATE	TOTAL	REPUBLICAN CANDIDATE	TOTAL	WIN-NING %
CONG. DIST. 1	BORK	108,086	†DOLE	113,212	51.2
CONG. DIST. 2	MONTGOMERY	77,189	†MIZE	80,806	51.4
CONG. DIST. 3	DIAL	54,522	†ELLSWORTH	89,588	62.5
CONG. DIST. 4	GLAVES	58,057	†SHRIVER	84,800	59.3
CONG. DIST. 5	RUSSELL	64,308	†SKUBITZ	83,120	56.1
KENTUCKY					
CONG. DIST. 1	STUBBLEFIELD		No Republican candidate		
CONG. DIST. 2	†NATCHER	78,582	BRATCHER	36,377	68.4
CONG. DIST. 3	†FARNSLEY	115,504	SNYDER	98,208	53.8
CONG. DIST. 4	†CHELF	88,058	MIDDLETON	58,895	60.0
CONG. DIST. 5	MILLS	48,547	†CARTER	58,983	54.9
CONG. DIST. 6	†WATTS	92,246	SWOPE	38,538	70.5
CONG. DIST. 7	†PERKINS	99,721	VAN HOOSE	43,220	69.7
LOUISIANA					
CONG. DIST. 1	HEBERT		No Republican candidate		
CONG. DIST. 2	†BOGGS	77,009	TREEN	62,881	56.0
CONG. DIST. 3	†WILLIS	52,532	ANGERS	31,806	61.2
CONG. DIST. 4	WAGGONNER		No Republican candidate		
CONG. DIST. 5	PASSMAN		No Republican candidate		
CONG. DIST. 6	†MORRISON	82,686	CRAWFORD	48,715	62.8
CONG. DIST. 7	THOMPSON		No Republican candidate		
CONG. DIST. 8	†LONG	33,250	WALKER	27,735	54.4
MAINE					
CONG. DIST. 1	CURTIS	95,547	†TUPPER	96,605	50.3
CONG. DIST. 2	†HATHAWAY	108,870	MacLEOD	67,044	61.9
MARYLAND					
AT LARGE	†SICKLES	668,166	SCULL	291,168	69.6
CONG. DIST. 1	HUGHES	35,235	†MORTON	39,439	52.8
CONG. DIST. 2	†LONG	135,355	PRICE	73,544	64.8
CONG. DIST. 3	GARMATZ		No Republican candidate		
CONG. DIST. 4	†FALLON	57,059	EVANS	16,512	77.6
CONG. DIST. 5	†MACHEN	122,724	POTTS	78,566	61.0
CONG. DIST. 6	HANSON	105,884	†MATHIAS	134,463	55.9
CONG. DIST. 7	†FRIEDEL	99,272	HOFSTETTER	25,374	79.7
MASSACHUSETTS					
CONG. DIST. 1	CONTE (R) won D. nom.		CONTE		
CONG. DIST. 2	BOLAND		No Republican candidate		
CONG. DIST. 3	PHILBIN		No Republican candidate		
CONG. DIST. 4	†DONOHUE	124,340	DUMAINE	45,644	73.1
CONG. DIST. 5	ARVANTIS	61,631	†MORSE	105,158	63.0
CONG. DIST. 6	ZAFRIS	71,212	†BATES	126,199	63.9
CONG. DIST. 7	†MacDONALD	117,550	HUGHES	39,027	75.1
CONG. DIST. 8	O'NEILL		No Republican candidate		
CONG. DIST. 9	†McCORMACK	100,849	MOLESWORTH	18,255	84.7
CONG. DIST. 10	DOOLAN	44,413	†MARTIN	85,785	65.9
CONG. DIST. 11	BURKE		No Republican candidate		
CONG. DIST. 12	BYRON	53,335	†KEITH	83,461	61.0
MICHIGAN					
CONG. DIST. 1	†CONYERS	138,487	BLACKWELL	25,565	83.7
CONG. DIST. 2	†VIVIAN	77,656	MEADER	75,954	50.6
CONG. DIST. 3	†TODD	78,163	JOHANSEN	69,519	52.9
CONG. DIST. 4	HOLCOMB	69,123	†HUTCHINSON	86,235	55.5
CONG. DIST. 5	REAMON	65,996	†FORD	99,704	69.4
CONG. DIST. 6	BENEDICT	65,704	†CHAMBERLAIN	85,238	56.5
CONG. DIST. 7	†MACKIE	95,252	SADLER	48,369	66.3
CONG. DIST. 8	BROWN	68,249	†HARVEY	83,205	54.9
CONG. DIST. 9	GRIFFEN	67,407	†GRIFFIN	96,956	59.0
CONG. DIST. 10	EVANS	66,582	†CEDERBERG	85,340	56.2
CONG. DIST. 11	†CLEVENGER	92,769	KNOX	82,452	52.9
CONG. DIST. 12	†O'HARA	125,805	POWELL	42,639	74.7
CONG. DIST. 13	†DIGGS	102,415	WATSON	16,587	86.1
CONG. DIST. 14	†NEDZI	186,815	BASHARA	59,485	75.8
CONG. DIST. 15	†FORD	103,824	FELLRATH	42,464	71.0
CONG. DIST. 16	†DINGELL	112,863	LEONARD	40,673	73.5
CONG. DIST. 17	†GRIFFITHS	136,180	HARRINGTON	50,580	72.9
CONG. DIST. 18	SIERAWSKI	74,681	†BROOMFIELD	109,677	59.5
CONG. DIST. 19	†FARNUM	88,339	KUHN	77,204	53.4
MINNESOTA					
CONG. DIST. 1	DALEY	87,781	†QUIE	108,639	55.7

(Continued)

MINNESOTA

STATE	DEMOCRATIC CANDIDATE	TOTAL	REPUBLICAN CANDIDATE	TOTAL	WINNING %
CONG. DIST. 2	SIMPSON	69,820	†NELSEN	97,803	57.7
CONG. DIST. 3	PARISH	94,682	†MacGREGOR	125,464	55.1
CONG. DIST. 4	†KARTH	144,801	DREXLER	54,221	73.5
CONG. DIST. 5	†FRASER	127,963	JOHNSON	78,767	55.0
CONG. DIST. 6	†OLSON	95,848	ODEGARD	89,228	51.8
CONG. DIST. 7	WICHTERMAN	81,718	†LANGEN	84,304	50.5
CONG. DIST. 8	†BLATNIK	124,277	GLOSSBRENNER	54,691	69.6
MISSISSIPPI					
CONG. DIST. 1	ABERNETHY		No Republican candidate		
CONG. DIST. 2	WHITTEN		No Republican candidate		
CONG. DIST. 3	WILLIAMS		No Republican candidate		
CONG. DIST. 4	WINSTEAD	29,142	†WALKER	36,592	55.7
CONG. DIST. 5	COLMER		No Republican candidate		
MISSOURI					
CONG. DIST. 1	†KARSTEN	137,442	FISCHER	41,232	76.9
CONG. DIST. 2	McCLANAHAN	112,786	†CURTIS	125,502	52.7
CONG. DIST. 3	†SULLIVAN	119,073	OHLENDORF	47,226	71.6
CONG. DIST. 4	†RANDALL	95,402	TAYLOR	54,587	73.6
CONG. DIST. 5	†BOLLING	86,821	LANGWORTHY	46,275	65.2
CONG. DIST. 6	†HULL	99,805	WURST	55,511	64.3
CONG. DIST. 7	THOMAS	90,114	†HALL	95,714	51.5
CONG. DIST. 8	†ICHORD	99,851	ROGERS	54,159	64.8
CONG. DIST. 9	†HUNGATE	95,810	SCHROEDER	56,196	63.0
CONG. DIST. 10	†JONES	67,199	PEINTER	30,700	68.6
MONTANA					
CONG. DIST. 1	†OLSEN	61,194	MONTGOMERY	52,422	53.9
CONG. DIST. 2	TOOLE	73,676	†BATTIN	80,956	51.4
NEBRASKA					
CONG. DIST. 1	†CALLAN	103,614	BEERMANN	96,551	51.8
CONG. DIST. 2	SWENSON	69,692	†CUNNINGHAM	77,986	52.8
CONG. DIST. 3	COLWELL	89,055	†MARTIN	100,162	52.9
NEVADA					
AT LARGE	†BARING	82,748	VON TOBEL	47,989	63.3
NEW HAMPSHIRE					
CONG. DIST. 1	†HUOT	78,942	WYMAN	75,109	51.2
CONG. DIST. 2	OFFICER	62,450	†CLEVELAND	62,687	50.1
NEW JERSEY					
CONG. DIST. 1	PROCACCI	103,546	†CAHILL	133,022	56.2
CONG. DIST. 2	†McGRATH	65,975	GLENN	60,926	52.0
CONG. DIST. 3	†HOWARD	103,869	DALY	101,787	50.5
CONG. DIST. 4	†THOMPSON	126,709	TOMLINSON	60,949	67.5
CONG. DIST. 5	FRIEDMAN	66,556	†FRELINGHUYSEN	113,185	63.0
CONG. DIST. 6	TRAYNOR	78,685	†DWYER	117,083	59.8
CONG. DIST. 7	IHNEN	79,012	†WIDNALL	97,027	55.1
CONG. DIST. 8	†JOELSON	111,301	MURPHY	53,849	67.4
CONG. DIST. 9	†HELSTOCKI	111,898	OSMERS	110,589	50.3
CONG. DIST. 10	†RODINO	82,109	SCHROEDER	25,552	76.3
CONG. DIST. 11	†MINISH	71,102	STUBBS	31,078	69.6
CONG. DIST. 12	†KREBS	73,043	WEINER	68,048	51.8
CONG. DIST. 13	†GALLAGHER	74,132	CASTALDO	20,828	78.1
CONG. DIST. 14	†DANIELS	60,107	WOOLSEY	20,200	74.8
CONG. DIST. 15	†PATTEN	129,106	RODGERS	75,827	63.0
NEW MEXICO					
AT LARGE	†MORRIS	193,280	SIMS	119,965	61.7
AT LARGE	†WALKER	165,003	REDMAN	154,231	51.7
NEW YORK					
CONG. DIST. 1	†PIKE	121,823	HART	68,134	64.1
CONG. DIST. 2	SILBERLING	73,588	†GROVER	75,738	50.7
CONG. DIST. 3	†WOLFF	72,212	DEROUNIAN	68,650	51.3
CONG. DIST. 4	MARINO (L) LEVY	74,364 / 6,090	†WYDLER	88,927	52.5
CONG. DIST. 5	†TENZER	88,615	EDSELL	83,466	51.5
CONG. DIST. 6	LEVIN	68,923	†HALPERN	88,385	56.2
CONG. DIST. 7	†ADDABBO (C) ASHEIM	101,216	NELSON	39,251	72.1
CONG. DIST. 8	†ROSENTHAL (C) HOSTEK	114,587	BREVETTI	33,053	77.6
CONG. DIST. 9	†DELANEY (L) RUDNER	96,200	COHEN (C) MARTIN	43,654	68.8
CONG. DIST. 10	†CELLER	92,410	HELD	12,443	88.1

NEW YORK

STATE	DEMOCRATIC CANDIDATE	TOTAL	REPUBLICAN CANDIDATE	TOTAL	WINNING %
CONG. DIST. 11	†KEOGH	46,858	SANDERS	11,395	80.4
CONG. DIST. 12	†KELLY	107,579	COLAVITO	21,984	83.0
CONG. DIST. 13	†MULTER (L) WEISBERG	108,122	HELD	29,153	78.8
CONG. DIST. 14	†ROONEY	44,467	TIRABASSO	13,510	76.7
CONG. DIST. 15	†CAREY	50,787	MARANO	46,604	52.1
CONG. DIST. 16	†MURPHY	67,597	SMITH	46,604	59.2
CONG. DIST. 17	FRENCH (C) O'DOHERTY	44,609	†LINDSAY	135,660	71.5
CONG. DIST. 18	†POWELL (L) LEWIS	93,681 / 5,017	BAILEY (C) SCHUYLER	11,656 / 658	84.4
CONG. DIST. 19	†FARBSTEIN (L) MORRISON	84,481 / 11,951	DEL ROSSO	24,901	68.8
CONG. DIST. 20	†RYAN	124,021	GOTTLIEB	23,237	82.6
CONG. DIST. 21	†SCHEUER (C) ROCKWELL	74,584	ROSE	12,898	85.3
CONG. DIST. 22	†GILBERT (L) MASUR	48,760	ROQUE (C) JOYCE	7,580	86.5
CONG. DIST. 23	†BINGHAM (L) HAGAN	101,535	FOLEY (C) LEE	28,639	81.3
CONG. DIST. 24	MALANG (L) BLOOM	45,300	†FINO	75,064	62.4
CONG. DIST. 25	†OTTINGER	110,351	BARRY	85,343	56.4
CONG. DIST. 26	CONNIFF (C) MITCHELL	79,595	†REID	101,462	54.7
CONG. DIST. 27	†DOW	91,906	ST. GEORGE	86,492	51.5
CONG. DIST. 28	†RESNICK (L) DAVIS	87,170	WHARTON	69,491	55.6
CONG. DIST. 29	†O'BRIEN	147,147	MEADER	62,872	70.0
CONG. DIST. 30	MARTIN	99,540	†KING	99,688	50.0
CONG. DIST. 31	BISHOP	59,040	†McEWEN	71,960	54.9
CONG. DIST. 32	CASTLE	76,571	†PIRNIE	88,299	53.6
CONG. DIST. 33	JOY	67,015	†ROBISON	95,869	58.9
CONG. DIST. 34	†HANLEY	90,764	RIEHLMAN	84,415	51.8
CONG. DIST. 35	†STRATTON	106,935	QUIGLEY	61,166	63.6
CONG. DIST. 36	WILLIAMS	81,566	†HORTON	106,186	56.7
CONG. DIST. 37	BUBEL (L) MACADAM	43,689	†CONABLE	64,026	59.4
CONG. DIST. 38	KELLEY	60,639	†GOODELL	84,391	58.2
CONG. DIST. 39	†McCARTHY	103,151	PILLION	89,640	55.5
CONG. DIST. 40	HILTS (L) PECK	58,352	†SMITH	76,154	56.6
CONG. DIST. 41	†DULSKI	131,027	KLAWON	29,210	81.8
	L – LIBERAL		C – CONSERVATIVE		
NORTH CAROLINA					
CONG. DIST. 1	†BONNER	52,567	RATCLIFF	11,108	83.5
CONG. DIST. 2	FOUNTAIN	62,406	No Republican Candidate		
CONG. DIST. 3	†HENDERSON	63,235	ROCK	30,557	64.1
CONG. DIST. 4	†COOLEY	73,470	GARDNER	68,387	51.5
CONG. DIST. 5	†SCOTT	72,254	ARMFIELD	67,781	51.4
CONG. DIST. 6	†KORNEGAY	84,151	GREEN	52,964	61.4
CONG. DIST. 7	LENNON	71,357	No Republican Candidate		
CONG. DIST. 8	JAMES	72,269	†JONAS	85,869	53.0
CONG. DIST. 9	DAVIS	71,629	†BROYHILL	88,195	55.2
CONG. DIST. 10	†WHITENER	78,684	YOUNG	55,483	58.0
CONG. DIST. 11	†TAYLOR	85,880	ROBERTS	55,996	60.0
NORTH DAKOTA					
CONG. DIST. 1	SINNER	60,080	†ANDREWS	66,034	52.4
CONG. DIST. 2	†REDLIN	58,011	SHORT	53,000	52.4
OHIO					
AT LARGE	†SWEENEY	1,865,865	BOLTON	1,711,918	52.2
CONG. DIST. 1	†GILLIGAN	74,104	RICH	68,834	51.8
CONG. DIST. 2	SAND	79,370	†CLANCY	121,928	60.6
CONG. DIST. 3	†LOVE	129,672	SCHENCK	119,315	52.1
CONG. DIST. 4	MIHLBAUGH	64,652	†McCULLOCH	81,284	55.7
CONG. DIST. 5	LANDIS	41,419	†LATTA	80,407	66.0
CONG. DIST. 6	SMITH	57,065	†HARSHA	85,524	60.0
CONG. DIST. 7	GRAHAM	71,918	†BROWN	92,350	56.2
CONG. DIST. 8	BENNETT	45,471	†BETTS	73,029	61.6
CONG. DIST. 9	†ASHLEY	108,678	CELUSTA	64,897	62.6
CONG. DIST. 10	†MOELLER	54,775	ABELE	49,765	52.4
CONG. DIST. 11	LAMBROS	81,197	†STANTON	99,409	55.0

(Continued)

STATE OHIO	DEMOCRATIC CANDIDATE	TOTAL	REPUBLICAN CANDIDATE	TOTAL	WIN-NING %
CONG. DIST. 12	VAN HEYDE	118,598	†DEVINE	146,817	**55.3**
CONG. DIST. 13	FREY	62,232	†MOSHER	74,776	**54.6**
CONG. DIST. 14	McGOVERN	104,537	†AYRES	126,145	**54.7**
CONG. DIST. 15	†SECREST	62,304	METCALF	31,862	**66.2**
CONG. DIST. 16	FREEMAN	93,137	†BOW	101,915	**52.3**
CONG. DIST. 17	LEVERING	71,146	†ASHBROOK	75,634	**51.5**
CONG. DIST. 18	†HAYS	93,640	DALRYMPLE	42,901	**68.6**
CONG. DIST. 19	†KIRWAN	111,682	JAMES	34,467	**76.4**
CONG. DIST. 20	†FEIGHAN	115,395	CIPOLLONE	39,558	**74.5**
CONG. DIST. 21	†VANIK	111,504	SMITH	12,290	**90.1**
CONG. DIST. 22	PATERSON	59,289	†BOLTON	80,473	**57.6**
CONG. DIST. 23	DENNERLL	66,008	†MINSHALL	135,660	**67.3**
OKLAHOMA					
CONG. DIST. 1	MARTIN	71,481	†BELCHER	123,434	**63.0**
CONG. DIST. 2	†EDMONDSON	90,399	LANGE	56,902	**61.4**
CONG. DIST. 3	†ALBERT	59,990	McSHERRY	15,608	**79.4**
CONG. DIST. 4	STEED		No Republican Candidate		
CONG. DIST. 5	†JARMAN	129,651	COWAN	53,444	**70.8**
CONG. DIST. 6	†JOHNSON	76,451	AUCHINCLOSS	58,216	**56.8**
OREGON					
CONG. DIST. 1	WHIPPLE	106,995	†WYATT	119,870	**52.8**
CONG. DIST. 2	†ULLMAN	69,355	THOREN	32,909	**67.8**
CONG. DIST. 3	†GREEN	148,302	DEAN	76,856	**65.9**
CONG. DIST. 4	†DUNCAN	121,823	JAFFARIAN	66,126	**64.8**
PENNSYLVANIA					
CONG. DIST. 1	†BARRETT	126,787	BELLO	50,334	**71.6**
CONG. DIST. 2	†NIX	129,178	HOWELL	29,881	**81.2**
CONG. DIST. 3	†BYRNE	110,076	POSERINA	42,627	**72.1**
CONG. DIST. 4	†TOLL	133,287	CAVANAUGH	74,419	**64.2**
CONG. DIST. 5	†GREEN	115,366	ROVNER	61,277	**65.3**
CONG. DIST. 6	†RHODES	141,676	BAMFORD	83,843	**62.8**
CONG. DIST. 7	BACHMAN	121,406	†WATKINS	126,261	**51.0**
CONG. DIST. 8	SAMUEL	105,834	†CURTIN	109,539	**51.0**
CONG. DIST. 9	O'BRIEN	80,255	†DAGUE	107,723	**57.3**
CONG. DIST. 10	HAGGERTY	83,134	†McDADE	87,839	**51.2**
CONG. DIST. 11	†FLOOD	113,821	THOMAS	34,370	**76.8**
CONG. DIST. 12	STEPHENS	54,545	†WHALLEY	77,622	**58.7**
CONG. DIST. 13	SEARLE	95,225	†SCHWEIKER	135,917	**58.8**
CONG. DIST. 14	†MOORHEAD	113,887	CAPOZZI	38,294	**74.8**
CONG. DIST. 15	†ROONEY	79,304	McCORMICK	40,291	**66.3**
CONG. DIST. 16	STEFANIC	49,372	†KUNKEL	87,251	**63.9**
CONG. DIST. 17	PLANKENHORN	64,541	†SCHNEEBELI	88,820	**57.9**
CONG. DIST. 18	REED	69,014	†CORBETT	112,965	**62.1**
CONG. DIST. 19	†CRALEY	80,860	GOODLING	77,681	**51.0**
CONG. DIST. 20	†HOLLAND	121,570	BRYAN	41,232	**74.7**
CONG. DIST. 21	†DENT	91,719	SCHOOLEY	46,791	**66.2**
CONG. DIST. 22	McCAFFREY	60,052	†SAYLOR	78,989	**56.8**
CONG. DIST. 23	STILL	61,313	†JOHNSON	78,854	**56.3**
CONG. DIST. 24	†VIGORITO	90,532	WEAVER	85,982	**51.3**
CONG. DIST. 25	†CLARK	118,573	LOTH	50,211	**70.3**
CONG. DIST. 26	†MORGAN	104,843	RIGGLE	49,837	**67.8**
CONG. DIST. 27	YOUNG	69,995	†FULTON	116,371	**37.6**
RHODE ISLAND					
CONG. DIST. 1	†GERMAIN	106,567	BLANCHETTE	54,385	**66.2**
CONG. DIST. 2	†FOGARTY	163,115	WELLS	36,862	**81.6**
SOUTH CAROLINA					
CONG. DIST. 1	RIVERS	56,162	No Republican candidate		
CONG. DIST. 2	WATSON	88,682	No Republican candidate		
CONG. DIST. 3	DORN	69,920	No Republican candidate		
CONG. DIST. 4	ASHMORE	81,727	No Republican candidate		
CONG. DIST. 5	†GETTYS	44,859	DOSTER	22,384	**67.3**
CONG. DIST. 6	†McMILLAN	49,398	KIRKLAND	26,586	**65.0**
SOUTH DAKOTA					
CONG. DIST. 1	MAY	92,088	†REIFEL	122,222	**57.0**
CONG. DIST. 2	BROWN	29,955	†BERRY	38,271	**56.0**
TENNESSEE					
CONG. DIST. 1	BRIGHT	34,236	†QUILLEN	86,266	**71.6**
CONG. DIST. 2	YARBROUGH	63,600	†DUNCAN	77,434	**54.9**
CONG. DIST. 3	SUMMITT	56,688	†BROCK	70,526	**55.4**

STATE TENNESSEE	DEMOCRATIC CANDIDATE	TOTAL	REPUBLICAN CANDIDATE	TOTAL	WIN-NING %
CONG. DIST. 4	EVINS		No Republican candidate		
CONG. DIST. 5	†FULTON	74,836	WILLS	49,290	**60.0**
CONG. DIST. 6	†ANDERSON	61,872	HILL	18,893	**76.6**
CONG. DIST. 7	†MURRAY MACLIN (I)	24,971	HURST	18,866	**50.4**
CONG. DIST. 8	EVERETT		No Republican candidate		
CONG. DIST. 9	†GRIDER	107,705	JAMES	97,724	**52.4**
	I—INDEPENDENT				
TEXAS					
AT LARGE	†POOL	1,608,931	HAYES	793,508	**67.0**
CONG. DIST. 1	†PATMAN	49,633	JONES	17,287	**74.2**
CONG. DIST. 2	†BROOKS	71,942	GRECO	44,257	**61.9**
CONG. DIST. 3	†BECKWORTH	52,795	WARREN	36,101	**59.4**
CONG. DIST. 4	†ROBERTS	46,538	BANFIELD	10,648	**81.4**
CONG. DIST. 5	†CABELL	171,381	ALGER	127,600	**57.3**
CONG. DIST. 6	†TEAGUE	50,165	VAN WINKLE	11,073	**81.9**
CONG. DIST. 7	†DOWDY	64,062	ORR	12,647	**83.5**
CONG. DIST. 8	†THOMAS	100,360	GILBERT	31,664	**76.0**
CONG. DIST. 9	†THOMPSON	102,508	OAKES	33,000	**75.6**
CONG. DIST. 10	†PICKLE	78,958	PRATT	24,354	**76.4**
CONG. DIST. 11	†POAGE	58,627	ISENHOWER	13,231	**81.6**
CONG. DIST. 12	†WRIGHT	96,112	DIELMAN	38,383	**71.5**
CONG. DIST. 13	†PURCELL	65,874	CORSE	21,398	**75.5**
CONG. DIST. 14	†YOUNG	100,278	PATTON	30,181	**76.9**
CONG. DIST. 15	†DE LA GARZA	59,916	COULTER	31,803	**65.3**
CONG. DIST. 16	†WHITE	70,286	FOREMAN	53,869	**56.6**
CONG. DIST. 17	†BURLESON	59,412	BRIDGES	17,567	**77.1**
CONG. DIST. 18	†ROGERS	55,783	PRICE	45,433	**55.1**
CONG. DIST. 19	†MAHON	83,956	PHILLIPS	23,973	**77.8**
CONG. DIST. 20	†GONZALEZ	100,464	O'CONNELL	55,993	**64.2**
CONG. DIST. 21	†FISHER	58,851	CLAYPOOL	16,824	**77.8**
CONG. DIST. 22	†CASEY	134,016	BARRY	96,367	**58.2**
UTAH					
CONG. DIST. 1	BRUHN	59,497	†BURTON	75,900	**56.1**
CONG. DIST. 2	†KING	149,897	JUDD	110,831	**57.5**
VERMONT					
AT LARGE	O'SHEA	70,726	†STAFFORD	91,966	**56.5**
VIRGINIA					
CONG. DIST. 1	†DOWNING	72,819	THIESSEN	19,698	**78.5**
CONG. DIST. 2	†HARDY	54,315	LUSTIG	17,082	**69.0**
CONG. DIST. 3	†SATTERFIELD HADDOCK (I.-D.)	43,880 39,223	OBENSHAIN SMITH (I.-D.)	43,672 939	**34.8**
CONG. DIST. 4	†ABBITT TUCKER (I)	53,857 23,682	No Republican candidate		**68.9**
CONG. DIST. 5	†TUCK	39,867	GILLIAM	22,946	**63.7**
CONG. DIST. 6	HOPKINS	45,113	†POFF	57,987	**56.9**
CONG. DIST. 7	†MARSH	47,887	ERICKSON	20,911	**69.3**
CONG. DIST. 8	†SMITH BAGLEY (I)	49,440 21,813	No Republican candidate		**70.2**
CONG. DIST. 9	†JENNINGS	51,106	WILLIAMS	36,668	**58.1**
CONG. DIST. 10	JOHNSON	78,242	†BROYHILL	80,370	**50.07**
(I) INDEPENDENT; (I.-D.) INDEPENDENT-DEMOCRAT					
WASHINGTON					
CONG. DIST. 1	PALMASON	73,901	†PELLY	106,184	**59.0**
CONG. DIST. 2	†MEEDS	82,199	WESTLAND	65,063	**55.9**
CONG. DIST. 3	†HANSEN	95,022	ANDERSON	37,866	**70.5**
CONG. DIST. 4	HUZA	49,844	†MAY	93,026	**65.2**
CONG. DIST. 5	†FOLEY	79,891	HORAN	66,422	**54.6**
CONG. DIST. 6	†HICKS	74,207	TOLLEFSON	65,500	**53.1**
CONG. DIST. 7	†ADAMS	113,635	STINSON	89,921	**55.4**
WEST VIRGINIA					
CONG. DIST. 1	BAILEY	73,151	†MOORE	116,198	**61.4**
CONG. DIST. 2	†STAGGERS	82,103	COX	43,699	**65.3**
CONG. DIST. 3	†SLACK	101,559	COMSTOCK	54,879	**64.9**
CONG. DIST. 4	†HECHLER	111,020	MILLER	69,264	**61.6**
CONG. DIST. 5	†KEE	74,270	BALLARD	32,144	**69.8**
WISCONSIN					
CONG. DIST. 1	†STALBAUM	90,053	SCHADEBERG	85,117	**51.6**
CONG. DIST. 2	†KASTENMEIER	108,148	KOLATA	61,865	**63.6**
CONG. DIST. 3	RISTOW	60,731	†THOMSON	89,534	**60.6**

(Continued)

STATE WISCONSIN	DEMOCRATIC CANDIDATE	TOTAL	REPUBLICAN CANDIDATE	TOTAL	WIN-NING %
CONG. DIST. 4	†ZABLOCKI	125,683	ESTKOWSKI	43,773	72.6
CONG. DIST. 5	†REUSS	107,610	TAYLOR	34,059	75.9
CONG. DIST. 6	†RACE	84,690	VAN PELT	82,106	51.0
CONG. DIST. 7	MARTIN	60,758	†LAIRD	98,110	62.4
CONG. DIST. 8	JOHNSON	65,292	†BYRNES	96,110	59.2
CONG. DIST. 9	BUCKLEY	86,071	†DAVIS	105,332	55.3
CONG. DIST. 10	NIX	71,983	†O'KONSKI	92,198	56.1
WYOMING					
AT LARGE	†RONCALIO	67,936	HARRISON	65,831	50.8
†Winning Candidate					

(H) HOUSE COMPOSITION BY ISSUES*

	Congressmen Who Support	Change From '62	Congressmen Who Oppose	Change From '62	No Stand	Change From '62
LBJ PROGRAM	210	+40	154	—28	71	—12
POVERTY PROGRAM	264	+29	150	—45	21	+16
MASS TRANSIT BILL	239	+20	172	—30	24	+10
MEDICARE BILL	218	+40	152	—37	65	—3

*Based on stands taken by the winning candidates

(J) HOUSE SUMMARY BY PARTY

	1964 D	1964 R	Change D	Change R	1962 D	1962 R	1960 D	1960 R	1958 D	1958 R	1956 D	1956 R
NORTH	117	80	+28	—28	89	108	92	111	103	100	73	130
CONN.	6	0	+1	—1	5	1	4	2	6	0	0	6
DEL.	1	0	0	0	1	0	1	0	1	0	0	1
ILL.	13	11	+1	—1	12	12	14	11	14	11	11	14
IND.	6	5	+2	—2	4	7	3	8	8	3	2	9
MAINE	1	1	+1	—1	0	2	0	3	2	1	1	2
MASS.	7	5	0	0	7	5	8	6	8	6	7	7
MICH.	12	7	+4	—4	8	11	7	11	7	11	6	12
N. H.	1	1	+1	—1	0	2	0	2	0	2	0	2
N. J.	11	4	+4	—4	7	8	6	8	5	9	4	10
N. Y.	27	14	+7	—7	20	21	22	21	19	24	17	26
OHIO	10	14	+4	—4	6	18	7	16	9	14	6	17
PA.	15	12	+2	—2	13	14	14	16	16	14	13	17
R. I.	2	0	0	0	2	0	2	0	2	0	2	0
VT.	0	1	0	0	0	1	0	1	1	0	0	1
WISC.	5	5	+1	—1	4	6	4	6	5	5	3	7
SOUTH	119	23	—4	+4	123	19	131	13	133	211	128	16
ALA.	3	5	—5	+5	8	0	9	0	9	0	9	0
ARK.	4	0	0	0	4	0	6	0	6	0	6	0
FLA.	10	2	0	0	10	2	7	1	7	1	7	1
GA.	9	1	—1	+1	10	0	10	0	10	0	10	0
KY.	6	1	+1	—1	5	2	7	1	7	1	6	2
LA.	8	0	0	0	8	0	8	0	8	0	8	0
MD.	6	2	0	0	6	2	6	1	7	0	4	3
MISS.	4	1	—1	+1	5	0	6	0	6	0	6	0
MO.	8	2	0	0	8	2	9	2	10	1	10	1
N. C.	9	2	0	0	9	2	11	1	11	1	11	1

	1964 D	1964 R	Change D	Change R	1962 D	1962 R	1960 D	1960 R	1958 D	1958 R	1956 D	1956 R
OKLA.	5	1	0	0	5	1	5	1	5	1	5	1
S. C.	6	0	0	0	6	0	6	0	6	0	6	0
TENN.	6	3	0	0	6	3	7	2	7	2	7	2
TEX.	23	0	+2	—2	21	2	21	1	21	1	21	1
VA.	8	2	0	0	8	2	8	2	8	2	8	2
W. VA.	4	1	0	0	4	1	5	1	5	1	4	2
WEST	59	37	+12	—12	47	49	39	51	48	42	34	54
ALASKA	1	0	0	0	1	0	1	0	1	0	—	—
ARIZ.	2	1	0	0	2	1	1	1	1	1	1	1
CALIF.	23	15	—2	+2	25	13	16	14	16	14	13	17
COLO.	4	0	+2	—2	2	2	2	2	3	1	2	2
HAWAII	2	0	0	0	2	0	1	0	1	0	—	—
IDAHO	1	1	—1	+1	2	0	2	0	1	1	1	1
IOWA	6	1	+5	—5	1	6	2	6	4	4	1	7
KANS.	0	5	0	0	0	5	1	5	3	3	1	5
MINN.	4	4	0	0	4	4	3	6	4	5	5	4
MONT.	1	1	0	0	1	1	1	1	2	0	2	0
NEBR.	1	2	+1	—1	0	3	0	4	2	2	0	4
NEV.	1	0	0	0	1	0	1	0	1	0	1	0
N. MEX.	2	0	0	0	2	0	2	0	2	0	2	0
N. DAK.	1	1	+1	—1	0	2	0	2	1	1	0	2
OREG.	3	1	0	0	3	1	2	2	3	1	3	1
S. DAK.	0	2	0	0	0	2	0	2	1	1	1	1
UTAH	1	1	+1	—1	0	2	2	0	1	1	0	2
WASH.	5	2	+4	—4	1	6	2	5	1	6	1	6
WYO.	1	0	+1	—1	0	1	0	1	0	1	0	1
NATION	295	140	+36	—36	259	176	262	175	284	153	235	200

NBC ANALYTICAL REGIONS

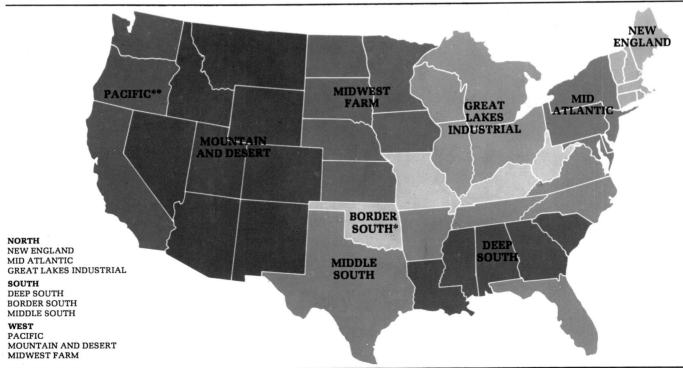

NORTH
NEW ENGLAND
MID ATLANTIC
GREAT LAKES INDUSTRIAL

SOUTH
DEEP SOUTH
BORDER SOUTH
MIDDLE SOUTH

WEST
PACIFIC
MOUNTAIN AND DESERT
MIDWEST FARM

*D.C. IN BORDER SOUTH **INCL. HAWAII AND ALASKA

The charts below (1A through 1I) show how various segments of the population contributed to the final totals of the 1964 voting. These figures were obtained from NBC News' "Electronic Vote Analysis" (EVA).

For two years prior to Election Day, NBC News had been feeding EVA's seven RCA computers with election statistics from over 5,000 specially selected precincts across the nation. Then, on Election Night, these established voting patterns were compared with the new returns from those same precincts to see if, where and how the patterns had changed. The information thus provided by EVA afforded a remarkably clear profile of how the electorate behaved on November 3. Never before has such a voting profile been available so quickly.

(1A) PRESIDENTIAL SUMMARY BY GEOGRAPHY
(IN PERCENTAGES)

	JOHN-SON 1964	GOLD-WATER 1964	% DEM. CHANGE FROM '60
NORTH	**62.7**	**37.3**	**+11.9**
NEW ENGLAND	73.4	26.6	+16.8
MIDDLE ATLANTIC	66.9	33.1	+15.3
GREAT LAKES INDUSTRIAL	55.7	44.3	+ 7.3
SOUTH	**54.8**	**45.2**	**− 4.8**
BORDER SOUTH	63.9	36.1	+14.9
MIDDLE SOUTH	56.9	43.1	+ 7.6
DEEP SOUTH	34.1	65.9	−19.4
WEST	**59.8**	**40.2**	**+12.3**
MIDWEST FARM	58.9	41.1	+14.5
MOUNTAIN AND DESERT	56.8	43.2	+10.5
PACIFIC COAST	61.0	39.0	+11.8

(1B) PRESIDENTIAL SUMMARY BY RACE
(IN PERCENTAGES)

	APPROX.* % OF VOTE	JOHN-SON 1964	GOLD-WATER 1964	% DEM. CHANGE FROM '60
NEGRO	**9**	**96**	**4**	**+19**
NORTH	6	96	4	+17
SOUTH	15	96	4	+25
DEEP SOUTH	12	98	2	+40
WEST	4	99	1	+14
WHITE	**91**	**58**	**42**	**+10**
NORTH	94	61	39	+12
SOUTH	85	47	53	−11
DEEP SOUTH	88	31	69	−29
WEST	96	58	42	+12

*In tables 1B, D, E, F and G, figures in bold-face type in the first column indicate what percent of the total **national** vote came from each category of voter. Figures in light-face type indicate what percent of the total **regional** vote came from each category of voter.

(1C) PRESIDENTIAL SUMMARY BY ECONOMIC BASE
(IN PERCENTAGES)

	JOHN-SON 1964	GOLD-WATER 1964	% DEM. CHANGE FROM '60
MOSTLY INDUSTRIAL[A]	64.1	35.9	+13.6
MOSTLY FARM[B]	57.0	43.0	+12.3
MIXED ECONOMY[C]	56.2	43.8	+ 6.2

[A]New York, California, Illinois, Ohio, Pennsylvania, Michigan, New Jersey, Indiana, Massachusetts, Texas, Wisconsin, Missouri. Ranked in order from most to least highly industrialized.

[B]North Dakota, South Dakota, Mississippi, Nebraska, Iowa, Idaho, Arkansas, Montana, Minnesota, Kentucky, Kansas, Wyoming. Ranked in order from most to least agricultural.

[C]Alabama, Arizona, Colorado, Connecticut, Delaware, Florida, Georgia, Louisiana, Maine, Maryland, Nevada, New Hampshire, New Mexico, North Carolina, Oklahoma, Oregon, Rhode Island, South Carolina, Tennessee, Utah, Vermont, Virginia, Washington, West Virginia

(1D) PRESIDENTIAL SUMMARY BY INCOME — OCCUPATION — EDUCATION
(IN PERCENTAGES)

	APPROX. % OF VOTE	JOHN-SON 1964	GOLD-WATER 1964	% DEM. CHANGE FROM '60
URBAN HIGH[A]	**15**	**36**	**64**	**+16**
NORTH	15	36	64	+17
SOUTH	15	32	68	+ 7
DEEP SOUTH	15	20	80	−11
WEST	13	34	66	+16
URBAN MIDDLE[B]	**21**	**64**	**36**	**+ 9**
NORTH	19	65	35	+10
SOUTH	24	65	35	+ 9
DEEP SOUTH	23	50	50	−19
WEST	22	61	39	+10
URBAN LOW[C]	**42**	**70**	**30**	**+11**
NORTH	47	69	31	+ 9
SOUTH	34	71	29	+11
DEEP SOUTH	31	51	49	−18
WEST	38	70	30	+14
RURAL	**22**	**52**	**48**	**+12**
NORTH	19	52	48	+16
SOUTH	27	49	51	− 1
DEEP SOUTH	31	25	75	−35
WEST	27	56	44	+16

[A]Income higher than approx. $10,000 per year; business or professional occupation; college graduate.

[B]Approx. $6,000-$8,000 per year; white collar job; attended high school.

[C]Approx. $5,000 per year or less; blue collar job; attended grammar school or no schooling.
U.S. Census Bureau definitions of "Urban" and "Rural".

(1E) PRESIDENTIAL SUMMARY BY RELIGION*
(IN PERCENTAGES)

	APPROX. % OF VOTE	JOHN-SON 1964	GOLD-WATER 1964	% DEM. CHANGE FROM '60
CATHOLIC	**25**	**75**	**25**	**− 1**
NORTH	32	78	22	+ 3
SOUTH	11	67	33	−15
WEST	18	80	20	+ 1
PROTESTANT	**71**	**57**	**43**	**+19**
NORTH	63	56	44	+24
SOUTH	88	58	42	+13
WEST	80	59	41	+22
JEWISH	**4**	**89**	**11**	**+ 9**

*Data derived from a public opinion survey.

(1F) PRESIDENTIAL ETHNIC SUMMARY
(IN PERCENTAGES)

	APPROX. % OF VOTE	JOHN-SON 1964	GOLD-WATER 1964	% DEM. CHANGE FROM '60
SLAVIC	**3**	**79**	**21**	**+ 1**
ITALIAN	**5**	**74**	**26**	**+ 1**
LATIN AMERICAN		**86**	**14**	**+ 2**
NORTH		74	26	− 3
SOUTH		97	3	+ 7
WEST		88	12	+ 9

(1G) PRESIDENTIAL SUMMARY BY POPULATION
(IN PERCENTAGES)

	APPROX. % OF VOTE	JOHN-SON 1964	GOLD-WATER 1964	% DEM. CHANGE FROM '60
BIG CITIES[A]	**23**	**68**	**32**	**+10**
NORTH	25	74	26	+12
SOUTH	10	47	53	+ 1
WEST	27	61	39	+ 9
THEIR SUBURBS	**18**	**62**	**38**	**+15**
NORTH	23	63	37	+17
SOUTH	7	56	44	+ 3
WEST	15	60	40	+12
OTHER METRO-POLITAN AREAS	**16**	**62**	**38**	**+14**
NORTH	17	66	34	+17
SOUTH	16	49	51	+ 2
WEST	13	59	41	+11
REST OF NATION	**43**	**59**	**41**	**+12**
NORTH	35	63	37	+16
SOUTH	67	49	51	− 3
WEST	45	60	40	+16
NATIONWIDE	**100**	**61**	**39**	**+11**

[A]The 35 largest cities in the continental U.S.

(1H) PRESIDENTIAL SUMMARY BY SPECIAL VOTE PATTERNS
(IN PERCENTAGES)

	JOHN-SON 1964	GOLD-WATER 1964	% DEM. CHANGE FROM '60	% NO PRES. VOTE
NORTH "FRONTLASH"[A]	**51**	**49**	**+21**	**5**
NORTH "BACKLASH"[B]	**79**	**21**	**0**	
NON-RIOT AREAS	83	17	0	
RIOT AREAS	74	26	0	
"BIBLE" BELT	**61**	**39**	**+12**	
APPALACHIA	**60**	**40**	**+15**	
"BLACK" BELT[C]	**33**	**67**	**−26**	

[A]The vote in selected high income-occupation-education precincts which are traditionally Republican.

[B]The vote in selected high ethnic precincts in cities which also contain a high proportion of Negroes.

[C]Counties with more than 65% Negro population but less than 5% Negro voter registration.

(1I) PRESIDENTIAL SUMMARY BY PARTY LOYALTY
(IN PERCENTAGES)

	JOHNSON 1964	GOLDWATER 1964	% DEM. CHANGE FROM '60
HARDCORE DEMOCRATIC AREAS[A]	**73**	**27**	**+ 1**
NORTH	76	24	+10
SOUTH	70	30	−14
WEST	74	26	+ 8
SWING AREAS[B]	**59**	**41**	**+ 7**
NORTH	66	34	+14
SOUTH	47	53	− 4
WEST	65	35	+13
HARDCORE REPUBLICAN AREAS[C]	**39**	**61**	**+16**
NORTH	50	50	+26
SOUTH	28	72	+ 8
WEST	40	60	+13

[A]The 5 most Democratic counties in each of the 9 geographical regions.

[B]The 5 most evenly contested counties in each of the 9 geographical regions.

[C]The 5 most Republican counties in each of the 9 geographical regions.

ASSISTANT EDITOR: MARY LYDON

ART ASSOCIATES: DOLORES GUDZIN AND SHEILA SMITH

ADDITIONAL PHOTOGRAPHS BY NBC PRESS DEPARTMENT—

SID DESFOR, ART SELBY, PAUL BAILEY AND FRED HERMANSKY;

EUGENE KOLOMATSKY; CHARLES HARBUTT (MAGNUM)

ELECTION CHARTS PREPARED BY I. A. LEWIS AND BERT IVRY

RESEARCH ASSOCIATES: MILDRED JOY AND EILEEN DWYER

PRODUCTION SUPERVISED BY EDWARD F. ANTONIOLI

PRINTED BY THE PHOTOGRAVURE AND COLOR CO.

TYPOGRAPHY BY EMPIRE TYPOGRAPHERS, INC.